Krystyna Szarzyńska

SHEEP HUSBANDRY AND PRODUCTION OF WOOL, GARMENTS AND CLOTHS IN ARCHAIC SUMER

T0151618

Krystyna Szarzyńska

SHEEP HUSBANDRY AND PRODUCTION OF WOOL, GARMENTS AND CLOTHS

IN ARCHAIC SUMER

AGADE 2002

ISBN 83-87111-22-8

CONTENTS

ABBREVIATIONS

Abbreviations used throughout this article are those of Chicago Assyrian Dictionnary (CAD)

Other abbreviations:

ASJ	*Acta Sumerologica*, Hiroshima
ATU-1	A. Falkenstein, *Archaische Texte aus Uruk*, Berlin 1936
ATU-2	(= ZATU) M. W. Green, H. J. Nissen, *Zeichenliste der Archaischen Texte aus Uruk*, Berlin 1987
ATU-3	(= LATU) R. K. Englund, H. J. Nissen, *Die Lexikalischen Listen der Archaischen Texte aus Uruk*, Berlin 1993
ATU-5	R. K. Englund, *Archaic Administrative Texts from Uruk. The Early Campaigns*, Berlin 1994
BagM	*Baghdader Mitteilungen*, Berlin
FAOS	Freiburger Altorientalische Studien
FSTW	H. J. Nissen, P. Damerow, R. K. Englund, *Frühe Schrift und Techniken der Wirtschaftsverwaltung im alten Vorderen Orient*, Berlin 1990
LAK	A. Deimel, *Die Inschriften von Fara, I – Liste der archaischen Keilschriftzeichen*, Leipzig 1922
LATU	= ATU-3
MSVO	Materialien zu den frühen Schriftzeugnissen der Vorderen Orients, Berlin
MSVO-1	R. K. Englund, J. P. Grégoire, *The Proto-cuneiform Texts from Jemdet Nasr*, Berlin 1991
MSVO-4	R. K. Englund, *Proto-cuneiform Texts from diverse Collections*, Berlin 1996

PI	S. Langdon, *Pictographic Inscriptions from Jemdet Nasr*, Oxford 1928 (OECT 7)
SEL	*Studi Epigrafici e Linguistici sul Vicino Oriente Antico*, Verona
SF (+ number)	A. Deimel, *Die Inschriften von Fara*, II – *Schultexte aus Fara*, Leipzig 1923 (number of the text)
ŠL	A. Deimel, *Šumerisches Lexikon*, Roma (1927, 1929, 1930, 1933)
ZATU	= ATU 2
ZATU (+ number)	number of sign in ZATU

INTRODUCTORY REMARKS

Information offered in this article concern generally the sheep husbandry and production of wool and artifacts made of wool in archaic Sumer. The conjunction, however, of this domain with other economic and administrative activities, makes impossible to single out the questions of sheep and wool production from the whole socio-economic life in ancient times.

The tablets from Uruk of Uruk-IV and Uruk-III periods (dating to around 3100-3000/2900 B.C.) form the basic source material for this study. They dominate in the whole corpus of the archaic Sumerian texts comprising nearly 5000* – in relation to *ca* 230 from Jemdet Nasr (see MSVO-1), 40 from Uqair, 27 from Larsa, and some others of mostly uncertain provenience being in the private or institutional possession (see MSVO-4).

In the archaic times Uruk was the single, big urban center in Sumer, surrounded by the large group of villages and settlements. Uruk was renowned for series of monumental cultic and administrative buildings. Its society under the leadership of the temple high officials/priests developed various branches of production and handicraft, and created a strong center of authority supported upon the system of a central administration. The development of the pictographic script, and of a stable writing system, which became a powerful tool for the bureaucracy – took place in Uruk. This writing system enabled the control of production and distribution of various goods (raw materials and artifacts, also animals), the hire of workers, the levy of tributes/taxes and offerings, and the like.

Similarity in content and mode of recording between Uruk and Jemdet Nasr/Uqair (Uruk III period – about 3000/2900 B.C.) shows

---

* The majority of them have not yet been published; some have been preserved only in fragments.

their close contacts with the central Uruk administration. It is why the texts from Jemdet Nasr and Uqair do not enrich our knowledge of the archaic Sumerian economy, particularly in the domain of animal husbandry and textile production.

Designations: "Uruk of the Uruk IV period" and "Uruk of the Uruk III period" are abbreviated to: "Uruk (IV)" and "Uruk (III)".

I present all archaic tablets and signs in their primary, i.e. "not-rotated" position. The original, natural position of a sign makes easier its recognizing and comparison with a real object. In ZATU and other modern publications, pictographs/signs are presented in their already "rotated" position (turned at a 90° angle to the left).

The comparison of pictographs with the prehistoric and archaic counters, so-called "tokens", used before and partly simultaneously with the early writing for the count of various goods, seems to be interesting and important for several fields of the ancient economy.

Detailed descriptions of several texts and problems, and numerous notes presented in this article, seem to be useful for the better acquaintance with the documentation, which forms the basis of each of the final conclusions.

CHAPTER 1 - SHEEP HUSBANDRY

Sheep and goats were the earliest animals domesticated in the Ancient Near East, already in the pre-ceramic neolith (dating to around 8500 to 7000 B.C.). The first information of the existence of the so-called "guarded" flocks derives from the archaeological excavations of human settlements in the west, north-west and also north-east regions of the Near East. Besides the respective animal bones, archaeologists have found a special "proof" originating from the seventh millennium B.C. namely a "token" identified later with the pictograph for sheep.[1] The flat, small disc bearing two lines crossing perpendicularly of its surface passes in the identical shape to the pictographic and cuneiform script as the sign for sheep or flock of small domestic animals. The reading for the sign is u d u (= "sheep") or l u g. The word l u g in the old Sino-Tibetan languages (affiliated to Sumerian) designates a pen/fold, in archaic times probably in the form of a circular for animals surrounded by a simple fence. Moreover, the word l u g can designate the very animals put into the circular.[2] The sign shape, which firstly looks as pure geometric and abstractive – thus difficult to explain – appears now as a picture of a round pen divided into four boxes to which various categories of animals were rounded up.

The sign/word u d u serves to designate a flock of a small cattle (sheep and goats) also in the Sumerian writing and speach

---

[1] See Denise Schmandt-Besserat: a) *Before Writing*, Vol. I and II, University of Texas Press, Austin 1992; b) *How Writing Came About*, ditto 1996; c) "Token at Uruk", *BagM* 19, 1988, pp. 1-175.

[2] Jan Braun, *Sumerian and Tibeto-Burman*, Warsaw 2001 (AGADE, 01-581 Warsaw, Krasińskiego 18 m. 252, Poland), p. 27: ŠL 537, 2/31 – l u g/l u k = "cattle and sheepfold"; l u = "to be put in; to lie (down); to camp; to encamp" (MSL II 151, 42 and 151, 43). Cf. Tibetan: *lug* = "sheep"; Archaic Chinese: *lôg* = "pen; domestic animal".

– we can find such a sign usage among the archaic accounts from Uruk and Uqair.[3]

The token mentioned above has been found in the site Beidha in Palestine, in the archaeological level of the seventh millennium B.C. – see token type 3:51⊕.[4] From later times we have only few similar finds, although the "UDU-tokens" were discovered in the South Mesopotamia and Elam – some of them dating to the fourth millennium B.C.[5] Other types of tokens appear in the course of the eighth and seventh millennia B.C. to count – in all probability – animals (without specification of sex and age). There are: a long cylinder ᶞ (token type 4:1) presenting "one" animal, and a simple circle/lenticular disc ⌒ (token type 3:3 or 3:4) presenting a "flock" (later used for the number "10").[6]

Thus we can assume that the domestication of goats and sheep reaches the pre-ceramic neolith, this process developed during the later period of time, and at the beginning of the sixth millennium B.C. the spinning of wool and flax was already known. In the Ubaid

---

[3] For example see tablets: a) W 9579dv from Uruk (IV), square Qa-XVI-2 (ATU-5, Pl. 77); b) tablet from Uqair (Uruk III period – see MSVO-4, No. 8, Pl. 4). See p. 17 in this article, Fig. 1 and Fig. 2.

[4] See D. Schmandt-Besserat, *Before Writing*, Vol. II, p. 408, token type 3:51. The token from Beidha has no parallel at that time in that part of the world. Therefore its presence in a seventh millennium level is difficult to explain and even suspicious (D. Schmandt-Besserat – personal communication).

[5] Tokens from Susa (Iran) and Tello (Iraq) are dated to the fourth millennium B.C.; other tokens from the south Mesopotamia (Ur, Uruk, Larsam) are undated, but, in all probability, they originated in the same time as those from Susa and Tello (see D. Schmandt-Besserat, op.cit., pp. 63, 193, 230, 266, 292).

[6] See D. Schmandt-Besserat, *How Writing Came About*, pp. 116, 119, 120 and 137 – token type 4:1, and p. 133 – token type 3:3. Cf. also *Before Writing*, Vol. I, pp. 151, C-152. The turning point for the further development of counting system was – at the end of the fourth millenium B.C. – the invention of numerals encoding abstract numbers (independent of the counted objects), as well as pictographs expressing commodities (various counted items). This new system ousts the earlier system of counting with tokens in "one-to-one" correspondence (see *How Writing Came About*, p. 118).

period the production of hides, wool and textiles is attested, and at least from the fourth millennium B.C. they became – besides grain – the main goods of Sumerian barter.

Numerous archaic texts from Uruk, Jemdet Nasr and Uqair demonstrate a high developed animal husbandry, especially of various categories of sheep and goats, less – cattle. These documents come from the last phase of the Uruk IV period (dating to around 3100-3000 B.C.), and from the so-called "Jemdet Nasr period" (3000/2900 B.C. = Uruk III period).

The quick development of cities and of the centralized and extensive administrative bureaucracy, caused the considerable enlargement of various kinds of production, as well as the need to control their delivery and distribution. In the archaic times that control was exercised by the special institutions / officials operating by the main temple (or various temples) located in Uruk in the precinct e š₃ named Eana. Deliveries, allotments, distribution of labor, services, etc. became objects of detailed account and registration. Some of the records are followed by special formulae designating the particular type of transaction, and sometimes by the titles of persons or names of institutions involved in this transaction or responsible for the counting.

Among the archaic texts dealing with domestic animals, we can distinguish five kinds of documents:

    A. records of one animal only (from Uruk (IV))

    B. records of various animals (from Uruk (IV) and Uruk (III))

    C. records of various goods, among others – animals (from Uruk (IV) and Uruk (III))

    D. herding reports (from Uruk (III))

    E. lexical lists (from Uruk (III))

First I will present the list of pictographs designating all kinds and categories of domestic animals appearing in the economic records, not only sheep – to make more easy the examination of the texts, in which various kinds of animals appear simultaneously. Beside some of the pictographs I demonstrate the adequate tokens:

Sheep

⊕	UDU	sheep/flock of sheep and goats (token type 3:51,⊕)
⊕	UDU+4 AŠ	sheep (four years old ?)
⊕	U₈	ewe (token type 3:54 ⊕)
⊕	UDU+NITAḪ	adult male sheep
⊕	UTUA	breeding adult male sheep
⊕	GUKKAL	fat-tailed sheep
⊕	GUKKAL.*gunû*	breeding fat-tailed sheep
⊙	SILA₄	lamb (token type3:14 ⊛)
⊙	SILA₄+NITAḪ	male lamb
⊙	SILA₄-SAL	female lamb
⊙	UDU-SIG₂	wool sheep
⊙	U₈-SIG₂	wool ewe
⊙	UDU+NITAḪ-SIG₂	wool male adult sheep
⊕	UDU-BA	sheep "assigned"
⊕	UDU-DUB	sheep accounted on the individual tablet

goats

⊞	UD₅	adult female goat
‡	MAŠ₂	adult male goat
+	MAŠ	male kid
⊚⊚	EŠGAR	female kid
‡	? (ZATU 421)	a kind of kid/goat[7]

---

[7] The sign ZATU 421 – its last form from the Uruk IV period: ‡designates a category of kid, attested many times in Uruk (IV). This sign appears often in the accounts of other kinds of sheep and goats, and sometimes it is summed up with all these animals on the reverso of the tablets, ending with the subscription: UDU-BA (= "flock assigned") – see tablet W 9579dv (ATU-5, Pl. 77), and p. 17 in this article, Fig. 1. In ZATU this sign has been included incorrectly to the sign-group No. 421 as a graphical variant of the pictograph NUN. In spite of the big formal difference between the both signs (‡ and ↕), they appear simultaneously in one entry on the tablet W 9656eh (ATU-5, Pl. 102), the fact which exludes their identity. Cf. remarks in ZATU, p. 129, a and p. 144, 5.1.

cattle

	AB_2	cow	(token type 15:3, )
	GUD	bull	
	AMAR	calf	
	AMAR-SAL	heifer	
	AMAR-KUR	male calf	
	AB_2-GUD	a category of cow[8]	

Pictographs designating various categories of sheep are the most numerous and differentiated in relation with other animals. This fact supports indirectly the high development of sheep husbandry, and the large range of their utilization already in the archaic period.

Examples of animal accounts:

ad A. Single-entry texts

From twenty-seven tablets of this type I have chosen seven well preserved, and characteristic in various aspects. They include records of various animals, mostly sheep (likely as the whole group of this type of documents). Single-entry texts indicate the early time of their origin (early Uruk IV). Twenty-one tablets came from a single find-spot – archaeological square Qa XVI-2, where the biggest group of archaic tablets (amount 450) were found together, among them – the most ancient. Three tablets were found in square Pd XVI-3 (not far the mentioned above), three others – in other sites, but also in the

[8] The meaning of the compound AB_2.GUD has not been yet finally explained, but it designates one animal, and only occasionally – the "cows and bulls". One of the signs appears, in all probability, as a genitive. Animals designated AB_2.GUD were counted by pieces (see tablets: W 9335c (ATU-5, Pl. 53); W 9579cc (ATU-5, Pl. 71); W 24156 (*BagM* 22, p. 137). On the tablet W 7227a (ATU-5, Pl. 26) on the obverso, in the series of entries we can see only various numbers beside the titles of persons/names of offices, and on the reverso – the total and information: GUD AB_2. If the numbers on the obverso concern cows and bulls, their names have to be specified in each entry on the obverso, because the economic significance and importance of each of these animals are extremely different and fundamental. See also CAD, p. 217 *littu*; moreover see Robert D. Biggs, *Inscriptions from Al-Hiba – Lagash*, Malibu 1976, p. 30, tablet No. 18 col. I : 1) "28" AB_2- t u r - t u r - a; 2) "2" GUD-AB_2; 3) "3" GUD-MU "2" (two years old) – here "two GUD-AB_2" designates undoubtly "two animals GUD-AB_2", and not "two herds of cattle".

region of the precinct Eana, dating to the early Uruk IV period. The following registrations are the most characteristic for this group of texts: a) place of transaction – Unug;[9] b) place of the stay or destination of the animal (e.g. in the simple reed pen t u r_5);[10] c) the sign

---

[9] The Sumerian word i r i / u r u oryginally was written with the sign UNUG (see P. Steinkeller, *BiOr* 52/5-6, 1995, col. 710 – note to the sign ZATU 583). In the archaic period this sign designates the precinct AB = e $š_3$, named Eana. Later on the sign UNUG designated the whole city, and finally – the city-state Unug/Uruk.

[10] The sign ZATU 416 ⬓ is identified by M. W. Green as NISAG, but this identification seems to be wrong. I read the sign ZATU 416 (= ATU-1 213) as TUR_5 = "reed-hut for cowpen" after Th. Jacobsen, "Note on Nintur", *Or* 42, p. 274. The pictures of cowpens with a bunch of reed stalks on the thatch, and often marked additionally with various reed-symbols ($MUŠ_3$, ŠEŠ, ATU-1 252, ATU-1 210 (= ZATU 323) are presented in the archaic glyptic and plastic arts (see below), and some of them also in the archaic script. The meaning of the sign ZATU 416 (ATU-1 213) as t u r_5 = "reed-hut/pen for a herd" can be supported by the fact that in many archaic texts the sign appears beside the names of various animals: GUD; $GUD.AB_2$; UTUA; U_8; MAŠ; UDU; $SILA_4$ (see tablets: W 6748b (ATU-5, Pl. 15); W 6760a (ATU-5, Pl. 15); W 9312g (ATU-5, Pl. 51); W 9335c (ATU-5, Pl. 53); W 9335h2 (ATU-5, Pl. 54); W 9335t (ATU-5, Pl. 55); W 9579bt (ATU-5, Pl. 70); W 9579bx (ATU-5, Pl. 71); W 9579dd (ATU-5, Pl. 74); W 9656ak (ATU-5, Pl. 90)). The sign of the reed-pen is recognized additionally in ZATU – sign No. 570 – incorrectly as $U_4.gunû$, because the sign belongs evidently to the group ZATU 416. The picture of a cowpen with bunch of reed stalks on the thatch and with the symbol-sign ATU-1 252 is presented on the tablet W 19408,44 rev., but this sign is not quoted in ZATU. As mentioned above, in the archaic writing and glyptic arts various reed-symbols (among others – $MUŠ_3$) were used to be placed on/by the pens in order to indicate – is all probability – their subordination to a specific owner, in that period – a specific deity or its temple administration. Only the sign with symbol NUN remained in use in later script to indicate a big pen named t u r_3. The disappearance of other sings of this group was probably caused by changes occurring in the husbandry organisation and the related record system. A very general meaning of the logogram NUN (= "prince, princely, lofty", etc.) mostly used as an epithet, could explain why this symbol survived in the sign $TUR_5 \times NUN$ (= TUR_3) to indicate the big pen for "sacred herds", without specification of its subordination to a definite administrative center. See K. Szarzyńska, "Some of the Oldest Cult Symbols in Archaic Uruk", *JEOL* 30, 1989, p. 4-5 and p. 9-Tab. 6; see also K. Szarzyńska, "Some Comments on Individual Entries in the Uruk Sign List ZATU", *ASJ* 18, 1996, p. 241, § 8, and p. 236; see also P. Amiet, *La glyptique mésopotamienne archaïque*, Paris 1961, seals nos 186, 230, 623, 632, etc.).

AN, which can be interpreted in different ways (among others, as the symbol of an administrative unit connected with the temple of the god AN ?); d) titles/names of professions known from other/later texts and lexical lists (for example: NAM$_2$-DI – (meaning not yet established); AB$_2$.KU read u t u l ("shepherd of cattle"); GURUŠDA ("butcher or slaughter place/house"). Not all of these additional notes appear in each of the mentioned texts. The following tablets from Uruk (IV) can serve as examples of the single-entry records:

    W 6760a (ATU-5, Pl. 15) – "60" U$_8$ TUR$_5$ ŠE-MAR

    W 9123b (ATU-5, Pl. 35) – "1" AB$_2$ AN ZATU 621

    W 9312,l (ATU-5, Pl. 51) – "14" GUKKAL AN

    W 9335b (ATU-5, Pl. 53) – "2" MAŠ SAL NAM$_2$-DI GURUŠDA
                                  UNUG

    W 9579bq (ATU-5, Pl. 70) – "60" GUKKAL EZEN×NIMGIR

    W 9579cr (ATU-5, Pl. 73) – "2" UDU+NITAḪ GURUŠDA UNUG
                                    UNKIN [ ]?

    W 9579do (ATU-5, Pl. 75) – "1" GUD AN UNUG AB$_2$.KU
                                    (= u t u l)

(tablets W 6760a and W 9579bq – see p. 17, Figs. 3 and 4)

Among the archaic single-entry tablets we can distinguish a special group of small tablets – the so-called "tags" bearing, among others, signs of various animals.[11] These tags are perforated, thus they can be hung on the horn of an animal or on its cord, and the like. They were used mostly in the case of animal transferred from one location to another. One tag – W 9656en from Uruk (IV) bears the sign GUD ("bull") and the title PA-RAD known from the most ancient lexical list Lú including titles and names of professions. The second tag – W 6759 from Uruk (IV) registers UDU (sheep/flock) with the complementary designation: IDIGNA (?).

The other tags come from Jemdet Nasr (see MSVO-1, 239 and 238, Pl. 89) – the first one quotes one male adult goat MAŠ$_2$, the second one – two goats MAŠ$_2$. The additional pieces of information indicate, in all probability, the consecutive transactions, moreover,

---

[11] The detailed description of the archaic tags – see K. Szarzyńska, "Archaic Sumerian Tags", *JCS* 46, 1994, pp. 1-10.

the first tag includes the formula ŠU-GI, the second one – the name of the god ^{d}Šu$_{2}$ (?).[12]

ad B. Registers of various species of animals, and sometimes – various persons/institutions

This group of documents represents the successive stage of the bookkeeping system, namely the common record of various kinds of animals on one tablet. We can distinguish above twenty tablets of this type, mostly from Uruk (IV), but from its later phase.

Some tablets from Uruk (III) are, unfortunately, badly preserved. As well preserved and representative I can quote the following records:

W 9312b (ATU-5, Pl. 50) – Obv. I-1) "[ ]" ‡ – kid (ZATU 421); 2) "1" GUKKAL; 3) "1" UTUA BA; II-1) "1" GUKKAL; 2) "3" UD$_5$ GA; III-1) "1" ⌜ŠU⌝; Rev."13".

W 9578c (ATU-5, Pl. 58) – Obv. I-1) "28" UTUA; 2) "14" U$_8$; 3) "203"$^?$ ⌜MAŠ⌝$^?$; II-1) "161" UD$_5$; 2) U$_2$-A$^?$ (subscript). Rev. I-1) "65" UTUA GA$_2$; 2) "74" U$_8$ GIG$_2$/GI$_6$; 3) "7" U$_8$; II-1) "10+?" UDU$^?$; 2) "5" UD$_5$. (note: the repetition of the sign of an animal in the several entries on the tablet is to be recognized as allotments of this kind of animal to various persons/units).

W 9579du (ATU-5, Pl. 76) – Obv. I-1) "4+$^?$" ‡ – kid (ZATU 421); 2)"5" UTUA; 3) "7" [ ]; II-1) "5" UD$_5$; 2) "2" EŠGAR; 3) "1" U$_8$ GURUŠ (subscript); Rev. "26" (total).

W 9579v (ATU-5, Pl. 64) – Obv. I-1) "[ ]" UDU+NITAH; 2) "2" GUKKAL; 3) "1"$^?$ UTUA, SANGA-UR$^?$ (subscript); II-1) "3" EŠGAR; 2) "2" UD$_5$; 3) "1" ⌜U$_8$⌝; reverso damaged.

MSVO-4, no. 8, Pl. 4 – tablet from Uqair: Rev. I-1) "8" UTUA; "1" UDU+NITAH; "4" UD$_5$; II – "13" UDU (total); MUŠEN KI GI (subscript).

(tablets: W 9578c – see p. 17, Fig. 5, W 9579du – see p. 18, Fig. 6, moreover MSVO-4, 8 – see p. 17, Fig. 2).

---

[12] The archaic single-entry tablets include sometimes also records of other counted items, for example: milk product (designated by the sign for a jar DUG); textile artifacts (ZATU 452-c); hide skirt LAL; fruits ḪAŠḪUR, and so on. But the number of these tablets is lower than of those with the animal registration.

ad C. Tablets from Uruk (IV) and Uruk (III) including records of various goods, among others – animals.

These tablets enumerate deliveries or allotments of various commodities coming from or destined to some persons/institutions. They do not offer any interesting information of the animal husbandry – records of offerings for the goddess Inana or for her temple to exclude.

In one of my papers[13] I have presented the lists of various offerings for the goddess Inana worshipped in archaic Uruk under three figures: ^{d}Inana - n u n (Princely Inana), ^{d}Inana - ḫ u d$_2$ (Morning Inana) and ^{d}Inana - s i g (Evening Inana). The offering sets differ from one another depending of their relation to one of these three Inana's figures. Princely Inana is known only from Uruk (IV), the related registers were found in square Qa XVI-2. The offering set consists, first of all, of definite quantities of grain, various kinds of bread, beer, dairy products, wool and some animals: one sheep u d u, adult male sheep UTUA, a category of kid ⚹, and swine (ŠAḪ$_2$)? The registers connected with Morning Inana originate from Uruk (III), and were found in square Pd XVI-3 (one in Pe XVI-5). The typical set of offerings recorded for Morning Inana consists of sheep u d u (in number 6 to 20 heads in one register), various kinds of food, silver and other not identified commodities. The registers connected with Evening Inana originate from Uruk (III) and square Pd XVI-4, they include several kinds of commodities, but – any animal. I present, for example the tablet W 6288 with offerings for Morning Inana – see p. 18, Fig. 7.

I can quote additionally the first position on the fragment of the tablet W 21446[14] in Uruk (III) with the inscription: "2" UDU AN MUŠ$_3$ AB, thus: "two sheep (for?) the goddess Inana (in/from) the precinct e š$_3$ (i.e. Eana)".

---

[13] See K. Szarzyńska, "Offerings for the goddess Inana in Archaic Uruk", *RA* Vol. LXXXVII 1, 1993, pp. 7-28.

[14] The tablet is published by J. H. Nissen, "The archaic texts from Uruk", *World Archaeology* 17, No. 3, 1986, p. 330.

In herding reports (see below) from Uruk (III), we can find two notes concerning, may be, the allotments/offerings of two male adult sheep UDU+NITAH for the goddess Inana or being her property in the herd, moreover of one animal (sign damaged) for the Evening Inana, and of one breeding sheep UTUA for/from the temple E₂.NUN (a g r u n ?) of the goddess Inana. The designations of some animals with signs ŠU and SIZKUR have a cultic significance (s i z k u r = "sacrificial animal").

ad D. Herding reports
This group of texts is especially important and interesting for our knowledge of the domestic animal husbandry in the Uruk III period. M. W. Green has distinguished forty-eight tablets of a common basic format, text arrangement and content concerning domestic herds.[15]
After author's statements:
"These documents are accounts of herds of domestic animals – sheep, goats and cattle. They are records of the number of animals in the herd, with adults and offspring tallied separately. Twenty-eight of the accounts deal with sheep, fourteen with goats, two with cattle, and one with sheep and goats together."[16]
The analysis of the reports made by M. W. Green in her paper, is very detailed and many-sited, based on autographs of all the related texts. Here I am restricted to repeat only the most important conclusions of this analysis:
"The animals evidently were kept together in flocks. – Flocks vary in size form, for sheep 22 to 140 adults with an average of 68. Goat herds tend to be smaller, varying from 10 to 50 adults with an average of 26. Two cattle accounts concern 2 and 4 cows."
"There are approximately equal number of males and females, occasionally more males. The natural female to male ratio suggests

---

[15] M. W. Green, "Animal Husbandry at Uruk in the Archaic Period", *JNES* 39, No. 1, 1980, pp. 1-35. (See p. 18 in this article, Fig. 8 – herding report W 20274,85).
[16] The remaining three tablets are too fragmentary to determine which species is involved. All categories of sheep quoted in this article on p. 6-7, appear in the herding reports, GUKKAL to exclude. This lack can be accidental taking into consideration a bad state of preservation of many tablets.

that the flocks were maintained for wool production, as confirmed by the occasional designation 'wool sheep.'[17] Reproductions rates are relatively low. For sheep the average is 40 lambs per 100 ewes, or 40 percent reproduction. For goats and cattle all preserved accounts show 50 percent reproduction – The corpus consists of three groups of accounts which clearly belong to a single genre of administrative document. – While the similarities among the texts outweigh the differences, and all probably belong to the archives of a central administrative institution, the three groups might represent either chronlogical stages or separate administrative offices. – The texts apparent designation of livestock for cultic purposes implies that they belong to a temple administration. Supporting evidence is the place of discovery: the Uruk temple complex. The rigid formalization of the accounts implies on often-repeated accounting procedure. As to the type and purpose of the accounts, they seem to be straightforward on the size and composition of single herds. They describe the condition of the herd at the end of the year."[18]

"Dairy produce is of only one type and is mentioned only after all other enumerations and compositions; thus the texts probably

---

[17] The word s i g$_2$ can designate also "woolen", and can refer to sheep especially selected for wool production, or indicate the best moment suit to obtain the rich fleece from sheep.

[18] M. W. Green in her interpretation of the archaic shepherd reports from Uruk (III) assumed the meaning of the term AŠ+UD 〈symbol〉 as the period of the year, according to Vaiman's suggestion (see M. W. Green, op.cit., p. 15). I interpret this term as the "first day" of the period the herd remains under a shepherd's care, i.e. – the period of the pasturage. The term AŠ+UD BAR in these reports concerns, in my opinion, the new-born animals (BAR = "additional, extra") in relation to the first day of the report, i.e. to the beginning of the reported period (which, nota bene, could not coincide with the full calendar year). The sign UD has its oldest and likewise fundamental meaning: "sun, day, shine", and so on, and it never has been used for the word/sign MU = "year". Only in later times the sign UD with the number "30" inscribed inside, has been used as the visual information "30 – days", i.e. one month (i t u d). The discussion concerning the interpretation of the sign UD + various numbers AŠ (from "1" to "10") – see K. Szarzyńska, "Archaic Sumerian Signs Indicating Succesive Days", in: K. Szarzyńska, *Sumerica*, Warsaw 1997 (DIALOG, 00-612 Warszawa, ul. Bagno 3/218, Poland), pp. 199-212.

do not belong to a dairy industry. Although the sheep are raised for wool production, there are not shearing accounts, since cattle are included and since wool or hair quantity is not specified for the sheep and goats. – While offspring are precisely registered, the reproduction rate is not outstanding; if furthermore, the term BAR is correctly understood as "extra", there are not reports from professional livestock breeders. What seems most likely is that a herd was given for one year into the care of a herder who had to account for all the animals belonging to the herd at the time of its delivery back to the administration at the end of the year. These would then be herding reports. – The three groups of accounts are authorized by the three different officials. For the simpler texts the official is the PA-NAM$_2$-RAD, for the most complex texts – the GAL-SILA$_4$, for the one text with the unique format, the NAM$_2$-ENGAR. All three titles appear near the beginning of ED Lú-A, but for none is correct reading known. It is only at Uruk in the archaic period that these persons are known to have functioned as officials. In later periods, the titles appear only in lexical lists and are absent from the economic documents."

It is noteworthy, that in the archaic economic texts the titles of shepherds of the herds appear very rarely. The title of the shepherd of cattle – u t u l (written AB$_2$.KU) appears in two archaic Uruk accounts – see ZATU 610, tablets: W 9656ag from Uruk (IV) – (see ATU-5, Pl. 90), and W 14361 from Uruk (III) – (see ZATU, Taf. 60), once with the additional title GAL, as in the lexical list Lú-A. The shepherd of flocks of sheep and goats termed later s i p a d (written PA.UDU) does not appear in the archaic economic texts from Uruk, but in the lexical list Lú-A of the Uruk III period, we can find the title GAL-PA.UDU, thus g a l - s i p a d "chief of shepherds". I think that in the archaic period the general term PA read u g u l a "overseer" was used occasionally as the designation of the simple shepherd profession. We can find in the archaic texts the title u g u l a beside the names of animals, for example: u g u l a – UTUA (tablet W 9655a – see ATU-5, Pl. 78); u g u l a – AB$_2$ (W 9656ex, ATU-5, Pl. 106), perhaps also u g u l a – GUD (W 9656ex, ATU-5, Pl. 106); u g u l a – UDU+NITAḪ$^?$ (W 9656hx, ATU-5, Pl. 113).

ad E. Lexical lists

Each of the texts called "Lexical list" collects numerous word belonging to one of various semantic groups. From the archaic time we can quote several earliest lists, namely: the lists of titles and names of professions (so-called Lú-A), lists of cattle, animals, fishes, birds, trees, wooden objects, plants, vessels, textiles, metal objects, food products, names of cities, and the like.[19] Sometimes one list consists of two parts, for example, the list of vessels includes in its second part the list of textiles. The lexical lists were created, first of all, for the scribal schools and for very scribes, but they could also serve as a material for the work on the further development of script and writing. The lists will be discussed here only in connection with the contents of the archaic records of domestic animals.

The archaic lists "Animals" (ATU-3, pp. 22, 89 to 93) quotes, among others, cow AB_2, bull GUD and calf AMAR, accompanied with some complementary designations. Interesting is the mode of designation of the animal colours, namely by the addition of the signs of items having one characteristic and stable colour: NE = "fire, flame" – for the brownish-red/rusty colour; UD = "day, bright" – for the fair/white hair; GIG_2 = "night/black" – for the black/dark colour; GI "reed, cane" – for a little motley colour. The same mode was used in archaic economic texts for the designation of colours of the pelt/hide, fleece, wool and textiles. In the list mentioned above we can find other designations of animals, among others: AB_2-ŠU and GUD-ŠU (compare animals destined for cultic purposes in the herding reports – see M. W. Green, op.cit., p. 8). Taking into consideration that tablets belonging to the lists "Animals" are partly damaged, we cannot be sure if they have not included names of sheep and goats – in any case such a list, for the time being, is not known.

The domestic animals are listed also in the list called "Tribute", discussed in details in ATU-3, pp. 25 and 26. Among the domestic animals the list includes "10" AB_2; "1" GUD; "10" U_8; "1" UTUA;

---

[19] The lists are published in ATU-3.

"10" UD_5; "1" $MAŠ_2$; "10" GUKKAL; "1" AMAR-GA (a suckling calf?/ a cow milk?); "1" AB_2-KAL (a cow grown up ?). The number of female and male animals are significant: "10" female and "1" male, i.e. the natural female and male ratio for breeding (see M. W. Green, op.cit., p. 11). Undoubtedly animals were used to be delivered by the citizens to the administrative units and temples as obligatory taxes/tributes or offerings.

In the list "Grain" (ATU-3, p. 144, tablet W 21916,1, Taf. 75) we can find terms: GUD-A; AB_2-A; AMAR-AB_2; moreover signs: SU/KUŠ-AŠ beside the animals: AB_2, UDU, GUKKAL and $ŠAH_2$ (swine).[20]

Below I present examples of texts discussed in this chapter:

---

[20] In the archaic economic texts from Uruk, Jemdet Nasr and Uqair the sign SU/KUŠ preserves the same, almost identical shape. In the archaic lexical lists from Uruk (III) this sign appears rarely, and rather with the meaning s u = "meat", cf. the list in ATU-3, p. 144 – "Grain"-D_2-D_6, in which we can see the compounds: SU/KUŠ – AŠ-AB_2; SU/KUŠ-AŠ-UDU; SU/KUŠ-AŠ-GUKKAL; SU/KUŠ-AŠ-$ŠAH_2$ (= "swine"). Taking into consideration that this list is qualified as a list of food products, I suppose that the sign SU/KUŠ in these compounds means rather s u = "meat", than k u š = "hide". The sign AŠ could be understood here as a designation "one year old". The sign AŠ under the pictographs of animals – see ZATU, p. 146, 5.4.

17

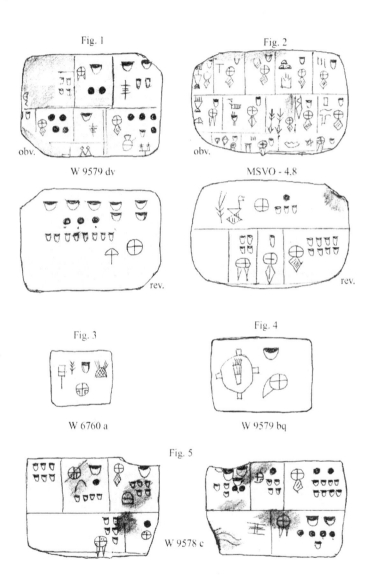

Fig. 1

Fig. 2

obv.

W 9579 dv

obv.

MSVO - 4.8

rev.

rev.

Fig. 3

Fig. 4

W 6760 a

W 9579 bq

Fig. 5

W 9578 c

Fig. 6

Fig. 7

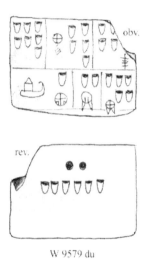

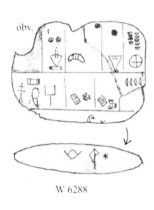

obv.

rev.

obv.

W 6288

W 9579 du

Fig. 8

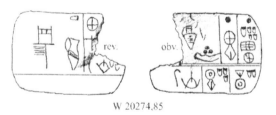

rev.

obv.

W 20274,85

CHAPTER II - RAW MATERIALS

A. Pelt/hide

The sign /▦\ SU/KUŠ read k u š had been used for animal hide, and later also as a determinative preceding all names of artifacts made of hide. (k u š as the determinative does not appear in the archaic writing).[21] Many information of the hide utilization as raw material for manufacturing various artifacts (for example: bags, sacks, garments, etc.) are known from later texts,[22] but the similar production might exist – perhaps in lower range – already in the archaic period. We know several archaic documents naming various kinds of hide k u š. On the other hand, hide and some of hide artifacts could be perhaps out of the central economic registration and control. The following terms concerning animals pelt/hide appear in the archaic records originating from Uruk (IV) and Uruk (III)[23]):

for sheep: k u š – b a b b a r – UDU+NITAḪ
             k u š – m a š
             k u š – GUKKAL
             k u š – s i l a$_4$
for buck: k u š – ŠEG$_9$ – NUN.

---

[21] The sign KUŠ appears as a designation for "hide, pelt" in the texts from Fara (sign LAK 293), moreover in the lexical lists from Fara (see A. Deimel, *Schultexte aus Fara*, p. 66 – list SF 64, col. VI, entries 6 and 7, and pp. 13-14 – lists SF 15 and SF 16 – in the compounds LAL-KUŠ beside the names of various animals). Cf. also ḪAR-ra = *ḫubullu* in MSL VII, Tab. VIII-XII, p. 123, among others: k u š - g u d; k u š - u d u; k u š – GUKKAL; k u š - m a š$_2$; k u š - u z$_3$ (UD$_5$), and so on. (In the list SF 15 the sign KUŠ was transcribed by A. Deimel k u š$_3$, but in this list it is written k u š).

[22] See A. Salonen, *Die Hausgeräte der Alten Mesopotamier nach Sumerisch-akkadischen Quellen*, Teil I, Helsinki 1965, p. 163 ff.

[23] See tablets from Uruk (IV), square Qa XVI-2, well preserved: W 9206a; W 9578d; W 9655ap; W 9579ci – in ATU-5, Pl. 46, 58, 72 and 84, respectively. Also see tablets from Uruk (IV): W 12119a+b and W 21278 (unpublished).

Moreover we can find two compounds of k u š with the title of the ruler/archpriest e n: e n - k u š; e n - k u š - u n u g; their interpretation is not clear, but – in all probability – they designate a special kind of pelt/hide destined for this high-dignitary.[24]

According to the later documentation, white hides of sheep and goats were preferred, especially to keep water, oil or other liquid produces. See: k u š - u d u - b a b b a r.[25]

A special interpretation of term LAL-KUŠ/ $^{k u š}$ LAL will be presented below.

The sign T 1 (LAL) ∧ in a sharp-angled form occurs many times in the records of garment/cloths of the both Uruk IV and Uruk III periods (over 50 times), mostly together with other typical garments/cloths.[26]

The pictograph preserves this form also in Jemdet Nasr and Uqair. In ZATU 307 – the sign LAL/LA₂ is presented as appearing only in the Uruk III script, in three various forms, but only the last one is identic with the archaic sign T 1.[27] In Fara period prevails the right-angled form (in the "rotated" position <), but in the economic texts and in the lexical list SF 16 the sharp-angled form occurs in both – rotated and not-rotated positions (see LAK 756; in SF 16 – ∧). In the list SF 16 we can find the series of entries beginning with the pair of signs LAL-KUŠ followed by the names of animals, among others: AB₂; GUD; AMAR; AM (wild bull); GUKKAL; U₈; UTUA; UD₅; MAŠ-KUR; SILA₄-KUR; MAŠ-GA; SILA₄-GA;

[24] See tablets from Uruk (IV): W 9168v and W 9578g (ATU-5, Pl. 41 and 59).

[25] See A. Salonen, op.cit., p. 164.

[26] Tablets with the registration of the skirt LAL are presented in Table II including the signs for garments/cloths from T 1 to T 38 appearing on the particular tablets.

[27] In ZATU the sign LAL is presented in the position "not-rotated" ∧ as the graphical variant of the pictograph ŠU₂ ∩ (ZATU 534), with the remark that the both forms of the sign can have different meanings in the textile accounts in which they appear sometimes simultaneously, in the different entries (see tablets: W 19408,46; W 20739; W 21026, and also the tablet W 21736). The detailed interpretation of the forms and meaning of these signs – see K. Szarzyńska, "Archaic Sumerian Signs for Garments and Cloths", in: K. Szarzyńska, *Sumerica*, p. 168 ff. The signs T 1 (LAL) ∧ and T 10 ∩ designate undoubtedly the different artifacts.

MAŠ-SAG; MAŠ-IŠI (mountain kid ?); SILA$_4$-IŠI, and some kinds of buck/caprines.

The form and meaning of the item termed $^{k\,u\,\check{s}}$LAL is not yet finally explained. In ŠL 481,52 the $^{k\,u\,\check{s}}$LAL is interpreted by A. Deimel as a designation/name of a furry skirt, named in Akkad. *aguḫḫu* According to the later data (see CAD, p. 159) *aguḫḫu* was an article of clothing, perhaps a kind of a belt or sash, and in the third millennium B.C. in paticular circumstances it was the sole clothing (see *RlA* 6, I, 1980, p. 23a). Many representations in the plastic arts of the beginning and the first half of the third millennium B.C. show persons wearing a large belt or a short skirt of pelt wraped up around the waist and hips. These persons can be recognized as high dignitaries, priests, warriors, once – a priestess-singer.[28]

I think that in the old-Sumerian and also archaic periods $^{k\,u\,\check{s}}$LAL indicated such a piece of pelt which could form a kind of a skirt. This, no doubt, important and vast spreaded clothing had to be the object of the profiled production and distribution – because it was recorded in the special textile/garment evidences, together with other garments and cloths. The whole documentation allows to accept the sign T 1 (LAL) occurring in numerous archaic records as a sign for the skirt discussed above. It is noteworthy that the sign LAL has other meanings: "to spread (out), to stretch, to extent" (ŠL 481, 50-a), which evidently harmonise with the shape of the sign LAL, and also with the fashion of the skirts presented in plastic arts (see p. 46, Figs. 9, 10 and 11). Among several statuettes, besides persons wearing furry skirts, we can see persons in sleek skirts with wisps at their lower end, that makes possible that these clothings were made of a tanned hide.[29]

---

[28] See p. 46, Figs. 9, 10, 11 (Fig. 9 – Philadelphia Museum; Fig. 10 – A. Parrot, *L'art de Sumer*, Milano 1969, Pl. 5; Fig. 11 – A. Parrot, *Sumer*, Paris 1960, p. 134, Pl. 163a).

[29] See p. 47, Figs. 12, 13, 14 (Fig. 12 – A. Parrot, *L'art de Sumer*, Milano 1969, Pl. 10; Fig. 13 – A. Parrot, *Sumer*, Paris 1960, p. 102, Pl. 130; Fig. 14 – A. Parrot, op.cit., p. 149, Pl. 178). The pictographs T 6 ⌂ / ⌂ and T 7 ⌂ showing the basic shape of a triangle, can be seen as somewhat similar to the sign T 1 ∧ (LAL); the dashes at the lower part of the signs T 6 and

Now I will discuss the meaning of sign T 2 ⋀, which – according to P. Steikeller's suggestion (op.cit., note to the sign ZATU 644) is to be recognized as TIL/UŠ$_2$.

I read this sign in the textile registers as s u m u n = "old, used". In these texts the sign appears always alone, in a separate entry following directly the entry with the registration of a definite garment/cloth.[30] Old clothings were objects of the accounts also in later times, cf. for example: t u g$_2$ - b a r - d u l$_5$ - s u m u n = "old garment – b a r d u l" (see *The Sumerian Dictionary*, Vol. 2-B, p. 120, 2.2) and terms: t u g$_2$ - g i b i l and t u g$_2$ - s u m u n, i.e. "new/old clothing t u g$_2$", in the ḪAR-ra = *ḫubullu* IX, §§ 205 and 206. Lack of the designation g i b i l in the archaic texts seems to be not surprising – in general only new artifacts have been recorded, and only in cases of old/used artifacts one might add the designation s u - m u n. The same situation can be observed in Jemdet Nasr texts.

It is difficult to indicate which artifacts demand removing hair/fleece from the pelt, but if you take into consideration the later data and variety of names of the artifacts made of pelt/hide, you must admit that this process had been known since the very early times. Undoubtedly several modes of gain the fleece from sheep and goats were known already in the archaic period (see below).

We can consider the similarity of the sign KUŠ with the token type 8:43 ⌣⋯⍿, although it is rather problematic. The sign LAL can be compared with the token type 8:1 △ .

T 7 can present the wisps ending the sleek skirts known from the monuments mentioned above. It is not unlikely that the signs T 8 ⌒ and T 9 ⌒ also present some kinds of skirts, however their semicircular shape is not as closely connected with the sign T 1 (LAL) as T 6 and T 7. Finally, it is impossible to say if those sleek skirts were made of hide or of a cloth.

[30] The sign T 2 ⋀ read s u m u n in the registers from Uruk follows the skirt T 1 (LAL) – 6 times, T 6 – 5 times, T 17 – once, and T 9 – once; in three registers the entries preceding the entry with the sign s u m u n are damaged – see Table III. In Jemdet Nasr s u m u n follows only T 1 (LAL) – as many as 15 times in 23 registers (see Table II and Table III). As mentioned above in the note No. 29, the artifacts T 6 and T 7, and possibly also T 8 and T 9, could present sleek skirts of hide or cloth.

If the signs T 6, T 7, T 8, and T 9 designate various sleek skirts with the wisps at their lower end, one can consider their similarity with the tokens: for T 6 – token type 10:4 or token type 8:7 ; for T 8 – token type 8:8 , and for T 9 – token type 8:29 . The sign T 7 shows an innovation in shape, which makes impossible to find an adequate token.

B. Fleece of sheep

Now I will discuss the problem of fleece gained directly from the plucked or shorn sheep, i.e. not being yet a clear wool s i g_2 / s i k i[31] fit for spining. The archaic sign for fleece has been not yet recognized. In later times the sign designating a fleece was BAR, ⌐ read b a r, the documentation of that translation causes no doubt. Already from the pre-sargonic period we know the designations: b a r-u d u = "fleece of a sheep", sometimes with the additional informations, as for example : b a r-u d u-s i g_2 = "fleece of a wool-sheep"; s i g_2-g i g_2-b a r-u d u = "black-wool fleece", b a r-s u-(g a)/b a r-s u u_3-a = "plucked fleece"; s i l a_4-n u-u r_4 = "lamb not (of an age) to be plucked";[32] b a r-g a l_2-l a = "unplucked fleece"; k u š-u d u-b a r-g a l_2-l a = "hide of un-plucked sheep", and the like.[33] The sign BAR does not appear in the archaic economic Uruk texts in contents connected with fleece, wool and textile artifacts.[34]

---

[31] In *The Sumerian Dictionary*, Vol. 2-B, the signs for wool is read s i k i, but in this article the sign will be read traditionally s i g_2, especially that s i g is the original sound of the word "wool" in the Sumerian (see J. Braun, op.cit., p. 52 – cf. *siṅ-ba* "wool" in the Old Tibetan).

[32] The compoud u d u - u r_4 is attested in Ur Archaic, see E. Burrows, *UET II – Archaic Texts*, Philadelphia 1935, sign No. 285.

[33] See *The Sumerian Dictionary*, Vol. 2-B, pp. 100-102, 4.2 and 4.3, and pp. 105, 119, 120 and 121.

[34] The sign BAR in the herding reports from Uruk (III), accordingly to the suggestion of M. W. Green, can be translated as "additional, extra" (see M. W. Green, op.cit., p. 6) in relation to animals born in the period of pasturage. In the texts from Jemdet Nasr the sign BAR appears sometimes together with the sign KID-b (ZATU 291 – three last forms of the Uruk III period), in the accounts of various items, as: sheep, skirt LAL, etc. (see MSVO-1, 96 (Pl. 35); 97 (Pl. 35); 99 (Pl. 36)). The sign KID-b

I found in the archaic texts from Uruk a sign T 37   ,   , not recognized, but clearly connected with sheep and wool. This sign does not appear in Jemdet Nasr and Uqair texts. In ZATU the sign is presented as a graphical variant of the sign $DARA_4$ (ZATU 73-c̲, although with reservations). I think that the sign T 37 cannot be included into the sign group $DARA_4$, even with regard to the formal criteria.[35]

T 37 cannot be seen as a graphical variant of the sign SIG_2 "wool", because in the Uruk III period the both signs appear already in their well shaped forms, in the same phases of script, especially in Uruk. However, both signs T 37 and T 38 – (SIG_2) show some formal similarity   and   , each of them associated of a ball/clew/pack of fleece or wool bound up twice.

The tablet W 21662,1 from Uruk (III) includes a count of a single item – T 37, which is apportioned in high quantities between various persons or institutions, among others, EN-SAG, ŠITA-NAM_2; SANGA-GAL, and the temple E_2.DUG_3-NUN; the total of pieces of this item amounts "2874", and was divided on the reverso precisely into four groups according to the colours: "1260" (pieces) of T 37 – b a b b a r ("white"); "551" T 37 – NE ("brownish-red/rusty"), "624" T 37 – DAR ("motley"), and "439" T 37 – GIG_2 ("black"). The same

can be translated, among others, as a ball/clew, thus the term BAR-KID-b̲ could be understood as "a ball/clew of fleece", or: "additional fleece". The sign BAR appears often in various archaic lexical lists, among others – in the compounds with the names of animals (see ATU-3 "Animals-7", tablet W 20266,53 col. I-3): ŠU BAR AB_2; "Animals 10", W 20266,53 I-4): BAR MUL AB_2; "Animals-61", W 20266,56 I-2): GI BAR AMAR; W 20521,3 II-2): X AMAR BAR). Because BAR has many different meanings, it is difficult to establish which of them was used in the compounds mentioned above.

[35] The archaic pictograph $DARA_4$,   ,   during the ED period had the form   – its meaning "dark" had been used sometimes to designate the colour of an animal, for example: a b_2 - d a r a_4, and in later periods also to designate a wild buck of dark colour of the hair. The reading and meaning of the sign $DARA_4$ – see P. Steinkeller, "Study in Third Millenium Paleography-3, sign $DARA_4$", *SEL* 6, 1989, pp. 3-7. A. Deimel in ŠL translated $DARA_4$, among others, as a dark-red colour or dark-red wool (similarly R. Borger in his *Assyrisch-babylonische Zeichenliste*. AOAT 33, Kevelaer – Neukirchen-Vluyn 1978).

designations of four colours have been used for animals, hides, wool and the clothing t u g_2 (see below).[36]

The sign T 37 is recorded also on other archaic tablets of Uruk (III) including registrations of various commodities. Two of these texts are interesting:

1) W 20274,1 – which in the first part of the obverso includes the account of "1380" sheep u d u for two persons/units, and in the second part of the obverso (separated of the first by the double line) – "3" products of the goat-milk (KISIM ?); "30" (pieces) of T 37, and one clothing t u g_2;

2) W 20511,1 – with the account of seven items: cow-milk (sign DUG_b – ZATU 88-b); "2" clothing t u g_2; "260?" (pieces) of T 37; "2" grain-products; "3" sheep u d u; and a quantity of cheese GA'AR. The account ends with the formula k u_2 = "for consumption/use."[37]

In both records we can find the same set of items: milk product, item T 37 and clothing t u g_2, moreover both tablets were found in the same square Nc XVII-1. Taking into consideration big number of sheep and item T 37, it can be not excluded that this set presents products characteristic for one big sheepfold located in or near by the square Nc XVII-1 (where many other archaic tablets were found, among others – herding reports discussed above (see p. 12)).

Other accounts of item T 37 are, as follows:

a) a fragment of the tablet W 24008,20 from Uruk (III) showing on the obverso the registration of "138" fishes SUḪUR; "60" (pieces) of T 37, and on the reverso – garments/textiles: LAL; s u - m u n; g a d a; T 16 (ME);

---

[36] In this text the not plain colour was designated with the sign DAR = "a motley feathered bird", instead of GI = "reed" used in other texts in relation to animals, wool, cloths.

[37] The meaning of the formula k u_2 – see Y. Rosengarten, *Le concept sumérien de consommation dans la vie économique et réligieuse*, Paris 1960, pp. 205, 206, 220, 241, 343, and so on.

b) a fragment of the tablet W 19568c including the entry: "40" (pieces) of T 37 – AN;

c) MSVO-4, 67 tablet (perhaps from Larsa) with the account of "10" (pieces) T 37 with ten various persons/institutions.[38]

d) MSVO-4, 28 tablet from Uqair, with the account of one (piece) of T 37, and subscript[?]: BIR$_3$-TE.

It seems to be convincing that the sign T 37 in the archaic time designated a ball/clew/pack of the raw fleece not yet prepared to the form of wool fit for the spining.[39] The archaic sign T 37 does not appear in the later periods of writing.

As instrument used to scratch the raw fleece (or wool) was a card presented by the sign UR$_4$ – ZATU 592 ⌇ , attested in Uruk (III) and Uqair texts. In the documents of Uruk (IV) this sign is not yet found, but it appears in the lexical list of Uruk (III) (see ATU-3, p. 176 – list "Unidentified 78x", tablet W 24206, col. II-4, Taf. 99) – in the compound: UR$_4$-BAR. In the Uqair texts the sign UR$_4$ is attested twice: a) in the term GIŠ-UR$_4$ (g i š = "tree, wood") on the tablet MSVO-4, 19, Pl. 10, including the registration of various commodities, among others – textiles: t u g$_2$ and g a d a; b) alone, as one of the products counted on the tablet MSVO-4, 26, Pl. 14, be-

---

[38] R. K. Englund in MSVO-4, 67 considers the possibility of another interpretation of the text, namely: "a consolidated account of female slaves (?) possibly assigned to the brewery represented by the sign ŠIM..., and to be traded (? sign ŠAM$_2$)". In that case the sign T 37 cannot present any counted object, but an element of the female-slave designation (name?). I think that as far as the archaic time is concerned, my conception of the text interpretation is more probable. In the case the item is the only thing counted in the whole document, this item can be indicated only in the first entry, without repetition in the following entries, and at the end of the reverso of the tablet.

[39] I consider the possibility to admit a very near meaning of the signs T 37 ⬭ (fleece?) an KID-b ▦ (ball/clew – see note 34), in spite of the fact that each of them is attested in the Uruk (III), and especially in the Jemdet Nasr texts. Taking into consideration the contexts in which the both signs appear, it seems that the difference of the meaning between them is not explicit, but the formal difference – rather distinct. The further speculation about the meaning and reading of the sign T 37 seems to be groundless.

sides various entries including accounts of various commodities, among others – T 1 (LAL) and T 31 (BARA$_2$). One can consider the similarity between the sign T 37 and token type 4:21 ⬚ or 4:29 ⬚.

C. Wool

Wool since the oldest phase of the archaic script and writing has been designated by the pictograph T 38 ⊕, ⊕, read s i g$_2$. This sign has its adequate token type 3:55 ⊕ or 3:56 ⊕ or 3:57 ⬚.[40]

The both – pictograph and token – base on the sign for sheep UDU ⊕. The tokens mentioned above were found in Sumer: one of the type 3:55 originates in Shibaniba (Tell Billa), and the four others – in Uruk. Token type 3:56 was found in Uruk, tokens type 3:57 – one in Uruk, and one in Nibru/Nippur, unfortunately all remain undated, but – in all probability – they derive from the early Uruk IV period, as the majority of marked tokens, so-called "complex", as well as the first pictographs.[41]

In the archaic texts s i g$_2$ "wool" can designate a raw material counted in records, or can be used in the attributive function, as an adjective or genitive for description of another object (for example: animal, garment).

In the archaic period wool as raw material was counted, like fleece, by pieces, in all probability by balls/clews of a conventional dimension.[42]

---

[40] I am inclined to recognize the double number of the criss-cross lines on the circle/disc SIG$_2$ as a visual form to underline the big value of sheep – as purveyor of wool – in the whole economy. Cf. the meaning of *gunû* in several signs.

[41] See D. Schmandt-Besserat, *Before Writing*, Vol. II, pp. 164, 202, 293.

[42] The analysis of the archaic texts shows that fleece and wool were counted "by pieces", but this "piece" can designate different objects: a) a ball/clew of a conventional measure (estimated approximately, or, for example, deriving from one animal), b) an unit of weight, not named – because it was well known as connected with the counted item. This unit was in archaic period one, and was recorded in the entire numbers. Since the middle of the third millennium B.C. wool has been mesured by weight (see A. Salonen, op.cit., p. 290-291, and *The Sumerian Dictionary*, Vol. 2-B, p. 100). The fundamental units were then: g u n = 30 kg 300 or 60 kg 600, and m a n a = 60 g i n$_2$

Four colours, the same as for animals, fleece and clothing t u g_2 were quoted sometimes for wool. In later times we can find designations: s i g_2 - p e $š_5$ - a = "a picked wool" (see A. Salonen, op.cit., p. 149); s i g_2 - ^{giš}g a - z u m - a k a = "a carded wool"(^{giš}g a - z u m "a kind of a special comb"); s i g_2 - u r_4 = "a shorn wool", and so on.[43]

Before the analysis of the particular texts, I will discuss the problem of the correct reading of the sign indicating wool. In ZATU under 452-a numerous signs with criss-crossing lines inscribed on their surface were recognized as graphical variants of the basic sign SIG_2. This sign presents a circle with two pairs of lines criss-crossing perpendicularly (in the not-rotated position), and only this form is to be read s i g_2 = "wool". On the contrary, sign-forms in ZATU 452-b, c and e designate various kinds of cloths/garments differing only in details marked with various numbers and arrangement of parallel lines inscribed on the sign surfaces (see below, Chapter III). The sign ZATU 452-d and some other signs of the group ZATU 452-a with many criss-cross lines, ⊛ , ⊜ do not represent wool or textiles. In the archaic records the related artifacts are counted under the numerical system ŠE used for grain and grain products, thus they must indicate some food products (see offerings for the goddess Inana, K. Szarzyńska, op.cit., p. 11, Table 1, Fig. 3; p. 14 § 2 and p. 22 – Table 3, Fig. 4; moreover see ZATU p. 133 c) and p. 134, and FSTW p. 71-72). In the offering sets for Princely Inana and Evening Inana the sign s i g_2 and the signs discussed above with lines crossing obliquely, are recorded separately[44] – these signs appear also in the accounts of food-products from Jemdet Nasr (see MSVO-1, 93, Pl. 33).

In the archaic texts wool appears in the accounts of various commodities, moreover in the offering records for the goddess Inana (see above).[45]

= around 505 gram, sometimes with the additional information: g u n - s i g_2 - a or m a n a - s i g_2 - a (i.e. the units used especially for wool).

[43] See A. Salonen, op.cit., p. 150.
[44] See K. Szarzyńska, "Offerings for the goddess Inana in Archaic Uruk", *RA* 87, 1993, Table 1, items 3 and 11.
[45] See K. Szarzyńska, op.cit., pp. 7-28.

Wool as a raw material appears in the economic archaic texts rarely – one can quote three tablets from Uruk (III) with the accounts of textiles, sheep and cheese GA'AR. There are:

W 20274,30 (ZATU Taf. 28); W 20274,45 and W 20494,4 (unpublished). The text W 20274,45 was signed by the PA-NAM$_2$-RAD – the official who accepted several times some of the herding reports (see Chapter I, p. 14). For the time being no one has found any account of the wool in Jemdet Nasr and Uqair texts.

As mentioned above, wool was quoted in four registers of offerings for the Princely Inana, see tablets: W 9206b (ATU-5, Pl. 46); W 9169b (ATU-5, Pl. 42); W 9579t (ATU-5, Pl. 64); W 9123ae (ATU-5, Pl. 38). In these registers the sign s i g$_2$ shows its typical form ⊕, but once – ⊛; they come from Uruk (IV), square Qa XVI-2.[46]

It is noteworthy that we do not find wool as an offering for the goddess Morning Inana and Evening Inana in the registers originating from Uruk (III). We know that between periods Uruk IV and Uruk III the important changes took place in archaic Uruk in its administrative organization, connected – in all probability – with some changes in the very cult (compare the deep reconstruction of the precinct Eana). It could be possible that also the set of cult offerings

---

[46] R. K. Englund in ZATU, p. 133-134, item c, and in FSTW, p. 77, considers the another meaning of the sign SIG$_2$ in the offerings records taking into consideration the bisexagesimal counting system used, among others, in the account (not offering register) on the small fragment of the tablet W 9656fm. I do not agree to that opinion, because in the offering registers the numbers appearing directly next to the sign SIG$_2$ are of the sexagesimal counting system used generally for wool. In the small fragment of the tablet W 9123ae (obeverso nearly damaged – one can read only the entry with the signs NINDA-BA), on the reverso, in one entry one can see four signs indicating the particular offerings, among them – s i g$_2$. The numbers in this entry are only partly preserved, and it is impossible to establish the counting system to which they belong, and if they present the total of the all counted items (in this place the surface of the tablet is not preserved, see ATU-5, Pl. 38). The other signs present, may be, the grain products. In such registers the right system of counting must have been used for particular item, and summing up the numbers of many different offerings – was in general impossible (for example: on the tablet W 9579t (ATU-5, Pl. 64) the totals counted according to different systems are separated). I maintain my opinion that the sign SIG$_2$ in the offering registers designates wool.

changed at the beginning of the Uruk III period (or, we have not yet found any related documents).

In the archaic records the sign SIG_2 in its attributive function appears beside the names of animals, mostly sheep (see herding reports: u d u - s i g_2; U_8 - s i g_2 UDU+NITAḪ- s i g_2).

In the archaic lexical lists the sign SIG_2 appears alone, in separate entries on six tablets included into the list named "Metal" (see ATU-3, p. 282). In fact, only in one of these lists – tablet W 21118, 1+4, (ATU-3, Taf. 68) the sign SIG_2 is explicit.

In the archaic list "Textilien" the sign SIG_2 is lacking. However, in later list from Fara – SF 64, from the column V-11 to begin, we can find series of entries including terms of several kinds of wool s i g_2 and of the clothing t u g_2 accompanied with the same complementary designations, first of all concerning four colours (white, black, brownish-red and motley), and with some other complements, for example: k u š - t u g_2 and k u š - s i g_2; ME - t u g_2 and ME - s i g_2; $BARA_2$ - t u g_2 and $BARA_2$ - s i g_2, and so on. The same designations appearing beside t u g_2 and s i g_2 can support the supposition that the clothing t u g_2 has been made of wool (see below, Chapter III).

In the archaic texts we can find only few data concerning the process of the wool-spining, weaving, as well as instruments used by these works. It can be supposed that in this so early period of the economic bookkeeping, records were restricted to counting only the incomes and expenses of the central temple administration. Registration of raw materials, artifacts, as well as their distribution among definite persons or institutions, does not include the middle stages of production, i.e. the works and items connected with the preparation of final artifacts. Yet the data from the sargonic and Ur III periods offer more information of the wool and textile production. It must have existed already in earlier times, also archaic, perhaps in lower range, and without official registration.

Some of the archaeological finds give proof of the existence of instruments used in the Ancient Near East in the textile production. For example, we know that for the spining only a simple spindle was in use, and for the weaving – only a simple loom.[47] These works were known already in the neolith – in the second part of the sixth millennium B.C.; the excavations conducted in Jarmo offered series of spindle-whorls and needles of bone used, among others, to sew together pieces of animal hide or textile. Whorls of looms originate also from the sites of Hassuna-culture of the sixth millennium B.C.

All these handicrafts developed and specialized in the following periods, also of Ubaid and Uruk. In Jemdet Nasr period spindle-whorls were made of a burn clay, steatite, etc., in the shape of cones decorated sometimes with simple patterns. Similar artifacts were found also in Tepe Gawra, and in the Ninive region, and in the South – in Lagaš region. The bar of the loom was made mostly of wood – see the determinative GIŠ beside the name of spindle: [g i š]BAL(A), Akkad. *pilakku* (see ZATU 46), but sometimes of copper (the whole copper spindle was found in Kiš). To fasten the wool-packet a special hook on the upper end of the spindle has been used. In the Lagaš period simple pierced pebbles were used to burdening the threads.

The archaic sign BAL(A) has been used later for spindle (the basic meaning of the sign is "to turn").[48] The archaic sign SUR/ŠUR, read s u r with the meaning "to spin", is attested only on the tablet of Uruk (III) – W 21554 (unpublished, see ZATU 498). This sign appears also in Jemdet Nasr ▽ (see MSVO-1, 17 I-1, Pl. 8).

---

[47] See A. Salonen, op.cit., p. 147 ff.

[48] The sign BAL/BALA in the Uruk IV period has the form ⚭ , and in the Uruk III period ⚭ , (see ZATU 46, with the note that the sign is attested on the tablets W 19416a from Uruk (IV) and W 22100,1 – from Uruk (III)). On the tablet W 9655aa from Uruk (IV) it appears in the compound with BAR (ATU-5, Pl. 82) in the subscript following the account of an unknown item. In Jemdet Nasr the sign BAL is attested once on the tablet MSVO-1, 234, Pl. 88 in the compound: [ ] NAGAR BAL SAG (n a g a r = "carpenter"); the word s a g beside BAL indicates, in all probability, its upper part, the so-called "head" of a spindle (cf. A. Salonen, op.cit., p. 154, 3): [g i š]s a g - b a l, Akkad. *qaqqad pilaqqi* = "the head of a spindle" ("Spindel-kopf"). The content of the text is not clear.

So limited number of names connected with the spining in the archaic period indicates the lack of the need to registrate the process and instruments connected with this work, but – on the other hand – the sign BAL(A) (which appears already in the Uruk (IV)) and SUR show that this work had been then known (the Sumerian scribes of the Uruk III period have inserted the sign BAL(A) 𒀹 into the lexical lists, although in compounds difficult to explain).[49]

The loom has been designated with the sign LAGAB (ZATU 308 ◯), which, according to Salonen's opinion, represents a rectangular frame of a loom. In archaic Uruk some special garments/cloths were inscribed inside the basic sign LAGAB, for example: T 16 (ME) and T 17 (𒀹, ZATU 753 – unidentified), see ZATU 315 and 321, as well as the archaic list "Vocabulary 9". The sign LAGAB in the form ☐ is attested in the Jemdet Nasr texts, twice in compounds with the item DUR counted on the tablets, and meaning, among others, "band, scarf, cord" (see tablets MSVO-1, 185 and 186, Pl. 73, and p. 73). The sign LAGAB could to be found probably also on the tablet from Uqair, but in a strong damaged entry, and its content is difficult to understand (see MSVO-4, 35, Pl. 20, and description – p. 23). In the archaic lexical lists the sign LAGAB appears in compounds difficult to interpret – see ATU-3, lists: "Tribute 71", "Practice-2", and "Unidentified 44".

In later times the name for loom was written: LAGABxŠERIM (ŠERIM = TAG, TAG means, among others, "to weave"), and also LAGABxŠE₃, or TAGxTUG₂ (literally: "to waeve (a textile) t u g₂.[50]

---

[49] See ATU-3, p. 111 – only in the list of the wooden artifacts "Wood-97" (ATU-3, Taf. 43) the last entry on the tablet W 24012,2 from Uruk (III) with the note: BAL(A) – BAL(A) – [   ] could be connected in some way with the spindle (the tablet is badly preserved). In other lists (ATU-3, p. 189) the sign BAL(A) appears in compounds difficult to interpret.

[50] Other names of spindle and loom parts do not appear in the archaic period (in the texts available to me), their quotation from the more later sources is not suitable in this article. See A. Salonen, op.cit., and other publications dealing with the manufacturing wool in the Sargonic and Ur III periods, among others, E. Waetzoldt, *Untersuchungen zur Neusumerischen Textilindustrie*, Roma 1972. See A. Salonen, op.cit., Tafels: LXXI, 2, 3; LXXII, 3, 4, 8; LXXIII and LXXIV.

CHAPTER III – GARMENTS, CLOTHS

Among the archaic tablets from Uruk we can find a group concerning records of various garments and cloths made of pelt/hide, wool and flax. The majority of them are not yet recognized. Their general meaning can be established because they are recorded together with the well known items of the same type, moreover, a few of them are sometimes summed up. There is a typological uniformity within the definite group of signs, which – in some cases – permits to suggest their general meaning (only products of the same type varying only in details, can be summed up).

All signs designating garments and cloths, as well as signs of fleece, wool, by-products of sheepfold, and also other ones unidentified, but appearing together with garments and cloths in the textile records – are presented in Table I under the symbols T 1 to T 38. Only signs indicating items of the complete different kinds (fishes, fruits, metal artifacts) even if appearing in the textile records, are not presented in Table I.[51]

All the tablets from Uruk, Jemdet Nasr and Uqair discussed in this chapter were presented in Table II, with data concerning their

---

[51] Similarity between some signs can suggest that they are only the graphical variants of the same pictograph. The difference of the meaning between the signs, in spite of their eventual formal similarity, can be established in the case when they appear simultaneously in one text – in separate entries. This way we can distinguish the following signs as independent ones:

a) T 1 and T 10 (tablets: W 19408,46; W 21026; W 20739; W 21736)
b) T 4 and T 5 (W 21026)
c) T 7 and T 8 (W 9578h)
d) T 7 and T 9 (W 19410,12)
e) T 18 and T 19 (W 19578b; W 19408,60; W 21278)
f) T 20 and T 21 (W 20274,80)
g) T 22 and T 21 (W 20274,80)
h) T 22 and T 23 (W 20650; W 19408,46)

provenience, and with the signs T 1 to T 38 appearing on particular tablets. The reading of the signs – if it was possible – was given by their numbers (in brackets). The signs are arranged according to their succession, in which they are recorded in the related tablets.[52]

It is noteworthy that in several records, beside the sign for the textile and its number, other signs appear in the same entry indicating persons or administrative units involved in the related transaction/account. There is no problem in the cases, in which these personal titles or names of institutions are well known – we can assume that they do not present any complementary description of the related artifact, but a different category of information (for example we can find the titles: KAB-NAM$_2$; ENGAR ("peasant"); NIMGIR ("intendant")-AN; ERIM ("warrior"); GURUŠ ("citizen"); SANGA-TUR; ŠEŠ-NAM$_2$; GA; GAL-TE; GAL-MAR; GAL-LU$_2$-GA, but also the title of the ruler/archpriest EN read en). In this last case, one should consider the title en as a genitive added to the name of the artifact to indicate its special kind/type connected with its destination for the dignitary en (for example, a better kind of material, a special fashion, finishing, and the like). Such a function of the title en can be supported by the terms appearing in the lexical list of textiles: T 18 – (tug$_2$)-en; T 8 – en; T 9 – en; T 20 – en. Only the stable compound being the complete name of an object can be included in the lexical list.[53] In the archaic economic texts from Uruk the title en appears beside the fol-

---

[52] Table II is based on 112 archaic tablets including records of garments and cloths. The number of tablets from Uruk (IV) amounts 35, from Uruk (III) – 46, they are completely or sufficiently well preserved. The number of tablets from Jemdet Nasr amounts 22, from Uqair – 8, one tablet is of unknown provenience. Some examples of the textile records are presented on the p. 45 – they are outline copies of the tablets from Uruk IV, Uruk III, Jedmet Nasr and Uqair. Numerous of the most representative textile records are not yet published, they are only quoted in this article, and in the Table II.

[53] See ATU-3, pp. 131, 132, the archaic lexical lists inserted into the list named "Vessels", items: 85 to 116, moreover some items in the lists: "Vocabulary": 2, 9, X, 6, and "Unidentified-47", and "Metal-56". The items inserted into these lists and referring to the textile artifacts, are presented in this article in Table IV.

lowing artifacts: T 1 (LAL); T 17; T 18 (t u g_2); T 20; T 22 – see Table II and Table III).

The second complementary designation appearing directly beside the clothing t u g_2 – is the sign BUR_2, moreover this compound is included in the archaic lexical list of textiles (see Table IV, entry "Vessels" no. 101).

The sign BUR_2 is used here for "a garment" (see *The Sumerian Dictionary* Vol. 2-B, p. 191). Other designations connected directly with the t u g_2 and T 25 ($TUG_2.gunû$) in the lexical list mentioned above, are the colours: black/dark, white, brownish-red and motley – the same as for fleece and wool; the sign $DARA_4$ "dark colour?" appears once beside the clothing t u g_2. Apart from the item T 1 (LAL) – b a b b a r "white" on the tablet W 21274,77 from Uruk (III), we cannot find any colour designation beside textile artifacts recorded in the archaic economic texts.[54]

The interpretation of the sign T 16 recognized as ME, causes some difficulty. The sign ME appears in numerous textile registers from Uruk and Jemdet Nasr, alone in the separate entry indicating a garment or cloth. In the texts from Jemdet Nasr we can find in a single entry the compound: T 16 (ME) – T 17. It is not clear if this compound indicates a different textile artifact, because the sign ME may also have the value i š i b – the title of a priest-exorciste or a "controller", and the same as the tittle e n, it can indicate a special kind/type of the artifact T 17. This compound T 16 (ME) – T 17 appears moreover on one tablet from Uruk (III), and on four tablets from Jemdet Nasr. One tablet from Uqair shows the compound t u g_2 – T 16 (ME) (see Table III).

The compounds of the signs T 18 (t u g_2) and T 31 ($BARA_2$) with the sign T 15 (AŠ), are also difficult to interpret. T 15 (AŠ) appears sometimes alone, in the separate entry, as a designation of a textile artifact, moreover – it can be understood in many ways. The sign

---

[54] See also the later lexical list from Fara – SF 64 including, among others, wool s i g_2 and clothing t u g_2 with the additional designations concerning four colours: UD/b a b b a r, GIG_2, GI and NE – the same as used for animal colours (see Chapter I, p. 15).

T 15 (AŠ) is often attached to, or inscribed into other signs, but it is very difficult to explain its meaning and function in those compounds, and its eventual influence upon their correct understanding and reading. The compound of the sign T 33 (a "rug"?) with the sign NA_2 "bed", can be understood as a coverlet for the bedding (see Table II tablet W 20493,1 and Table III – sign T 33).

The adjective g a l ("big, grand, great") appears once beside the artifact made of flax (T 3 (g a d a)), and the word s a g designating probably the "first class" – accompanies the artifact T 30 (see tablets W 24012,4 and MSVO-4, 26, Pl. 14 in the Table II; W 24024,1).

Taking into consideration the subject of this article, I will present more precisely garments and cloths made of wool.

The woolen artifacts are presented by the series of typologically connected signs, which were composed on the basic shape of a circle/disc connected, undoubtedly, with the sign for sheep u d u and wool s i g_2, and explicitly connected with the sign T 18 ⬭ recognized as a textile/clothing t u g_2. In the archaic times the word t u g_2 designates a piece of woolen textile/material used as a simple, upper clothing put on the skirt and the whole body through the left shoulder, and bind in the line of hips.[55] This clothing is most often counted in the textile records, and it is the most spread in use in archaic times. It is why the sign and the word t u g_2 became later the determinative preceding all the names of garments/cloths. In the archaic times t u g_2 was counted by pieces, each of them probably of a conventional dimension.

The signs for woolen garments/cloths are, as follows:

T 18	- t u g_2	⬭,	token type 3:28[56]	⬭
T 19	- unidentified	⬭,	" " 3:20/29	⬭, ⬭
T 20	- idem	⬭, ⬭,	" " 3:21/30	⬭

---

[55] See p. 48, Figs. 15, 16, 17 (Fig. 15 – Iraq Museum; Fig. 16 – Iraq Museum; Fig. 17 – a fragment of the so-called "Stele of Eanatum", A. Parrot, *Sumer*, Paris 1960, p. 135, Pl. 164).

[56] See D. Schmandt-Besserat, *How Writing Came About*, pp. 134, 135. The small circle on the disc indicates the disc perforation used to string the token; this circle/perforation is not significant for the meaning of the token.

T 21	- idem	◐ ,	token type	3:32/33	◉
T 22	- idem	◑ ,	" "	3:22/24	◍
T 23	- idem	◉ ,	" "	3:24/25	◍
T 24	- idem	⍟ ,	–		
T 25	- idem	◐ ,	token type	3:39?	◉
T 26	- idem	⍟ ,	–		

From T 18 to T 23 the signs differ only in number and arrangement of parallel, vertical lines inscribed on the circle/disc. These parallel lines from number three upwards can represent the "multiplication" of two lines appearing in the sign T 18 (t u g$_2$), and indicating a piece of cloth made, in all probability, of wool (thus the signs ZATU 452-b̲,-c̲ and -e̲ indicate also artifacts made of wool).

The number of lines on the surface of the signs is not accidental, because in several records we can see signs with various numbers of lines appearing simultaneously in separate entries, in the same text (for example tablets: W 19408,46; W 19408,60; W 19684,a; W 20274, 80; W 20650; W 21671 (these tablets are not yet published), and W 21278 (see FAOS 3, 1979, Taf. 30). Apart from the sign T 18 (t u g$_2$) other signs (T 19 to T 23) are not yet recognized and read. In ZATU these signs are presented as graphical variants of the sign T 38 (SIG$_2$) = "wool", but this interpretation is not correct (see Chapter II p. 28).

Other signs of this group are presented in ZATU only in a descriptive manner, i.e. T 24 as TUG$_2$+BAD+BAD, T 25 – as TUG$_2$.gunû, and T 26 – as TUG$_2$.gunû+BAD+BAD. Such a description cannot be accepted as the reading, because very often compounds have the different reading than their particular signs. As it has been showed in the note no. 51, the signs for garments/cloths T 18 and T 19, T 20 and T 21, T 22 and T 21, T 22 and T 23 represent different artifacts.

The sign T 18 (t u g$_2$) – is attested most often – on the whole in the 81 registers it appears 28 times alone, in the separate entries (apart from the compounds mentioned above – see p. 34-35). On the contrary in Jemdet Nasr in 22 registers the clothing t u g$_2$ appears only three times, in Uqair in 8 registers – four times.

It is to be stressed that in archaic Uruk the designation s u - m u n does not follow the clothing t u g_2, contrary as in the case of T 1 (LAL). In archaic Uruk s u m u n follows T 1 (LAL) six times, T 6 – five times, T 9 – once, and T 17 – once. The same situation takes place in Jemdet Nasr – the skirt T 1 (LAL) with following s u m u n appears generally (fifteen times in twenty two registers), the clothing t u g_2 – any time. It looks that the skirts of pelt/hide were sufficiently fast to be used again, on the contrary than the textiles of wool or flax.

In the Uruk IV period the artifact t u g_2 was designated only by the single sign T 18 (t u g_2 - e n to exlude).

In the Uruk III period several differentiations appear in the designation for t u g_2, in the form of the addition of various other signs to the single sign t u g_2 (the most frequent are the additional signs BUR_2 and AŠ, see Table III).

The almost total lack of the accounts of the clothing t u g_2 in Jemdet Nasr is very surprising (see above, and Table III). This situation, however, could be seen as accidental, caused by the small number and bad state of preservation of documents originating from Jemdet Nasr, especially that near by in Uqair the artifact t u g_2 appears often (four times in eight registers). After all, it looks as if in Jemdet Nasr the skirt T 1 (LAL) was the main garment – new or old – counted in the registers.

The signs T 24 𝍩 and T 26 𝍩 remain not recognized – neither their reading, nor their meaning, although they are connected in some way with the textiles t u g_2 and $TUG_2.gunû$, respectively.

The signs BAD-BAD, Akkad. *tapatu* designates, among others, a kind of cloth or garment, but its correct recognition is not yet possible. The sign T 24 appears in the Uruk (III) texts as many as ten times, the sign T 26 – only twice. T 25 𝍩 seems to be connected with the signs T 18 (t u g_2), in ZATU it is described as $TUG_2.gunû$, thus the clothing t u g_2 with a supplementary qualitative characteristic. The sign is attested only in two texts from Uruk (III), in Jemdet Nasr and Uqair it is absent.

One cannot say anything concrete about the signs T 19 to T 23, only that they are artifacts of similar type as the clothing t u g_2 – what results from their shape and presence in the textile records. After the analysis of the signs T 18 (t u g_2) to T 23, and T 25, it can be assumed that the differences between respective textile artifacts rely on the various kinds of material, for example – various thickness and twist of threads or different mode of weaving – these elements can give different patterns on the textile, its thickness, ways of using, and the like. It is, of course, a hypothesis, but in my opinion – very probable.

In any case, the distribution of the textile artifacts subjected to an official control exercised by the central economic administrative office(s). First these artifacts must have been delivered by the weavers to a special economic centres/storehouses, and further – distributed between various persons/institutions. We cannot say if the textile production carried out apart the central institutions, to supply people's wants, but I think it is very probable. The numbers of the registered artifacts, and the titles of dignitaries and officials appearing in the textile registers indicate rather the fact that only those persons have received allotments of garments/cloths directly from the economic – administrative offices.

The artifacts designated with the signs: T 31, T 32, T 33 and T 34 can be discussed together. These signs, similar in shape, appear in the typical textile accounts. Among these signs only T 31 is recognized and read BARA$_2$, its meaning is, among others, "bag, sack"; this artifact could be made of hide or textile. Because in the archaic times there are no determinatives and detailed descriptions – we do not know anything about the material this type of bag/sack have been made of. The sign T 31 (BARA$_2$) appears relatively often in the both archaic periods: in Uruk IV – four times, in Uruk III – eleven times, twice with the additional sign T 15 (AŠ). It was recorded once in the tablet from Uqair (MSVO-4, 26, Pl. 14) together with the sign DUR$_2$.

Other signs of this group are attested: T 32 once in Uruk (IV); T 33 – five times in Uruk (III); T 34 – once in Uruk

(III).[57] It should be stressed that the similarity of the signs T 32, T 33 and T 34 with the sign T 31 – BARA$_2$ = "sack, bag" can be only formal, and these signs could not have the meaning similar BARA$_2$.

On the other hand, taking into consideration that the sign T 33 appears together with the sign NA$_2$ it can indicate a coverlet or a "rug".

I think that all we can say that mentioned artifacts were woven, and it is why they were counted together with other textile artifacts (provided that they were made of hide).

We can find tokens, which can be compared with the signs of "bags/rugs", namely:

T 31 (BARA$_2$) – with the token type 7:17 ⬚ ; sign T 32 – with the token type 7:18 ▣ ; T 33 – with token type 7:5 ▣ (see Table I).

The following signs appear in the textile evidences of Uruk (III) presenting by/products of sheepfolds:

1) T 27 ▷◁ recognized by R. K. Englund as a sign for small cheeses named GA AR, and counted according to the sexagesimal system of counting (see ZATU p. 134,d, and FSTW p. 135). These products had been registered sometimes in very high quantities. The sign appears on five tablets from Uruk (III).

---

[57] The pictograph T 34 ▣ is a bit like the sign ZATU 291 – but only its first form coming from the Uruk III period, without the small dash, which appears in T 34. This sign is included in ZATU to the group of signs read KID, but in my opinion – incorrectly. Three other forms presented in ZATU, (sign-group 291 of Uruk III period ▤) are completely different in shape from the first form mentioned above. These three signs can be recognized as KID. In my opinion the first form of the sign ZATU 291 of Uruk III period cannot be associated with the signs read KID. The sign T 34 appears in some of the archaic lexical lists in the shape almost identical as that found in Uruk (see ATU-3, p. 246 ▦ – without the small dash, and tablets: W 21208,49 (Taf. 32) and W 20335,3 (Taf. 81), but we cannot say anything more about its meaning and reading. In Jemdet Nasr another sign a bit like T 34 ▣ is attested on four tablets, but in subscripts, and not as a counted item (see MSVO-1, 94, 95, 115 and 185, Pl. 34, 44 and 73). The second sign from Jemdet Nasr in the form ▥ , also similar to T 34, appears on the tablet MSVO-1, 107, Pl. 38, but also in subscript, and not as a counted item. Hovewer, we cannot exclude that the signs from Jemdet Nasr represent a local form of the sign T 34, as well as the first form of the sign ZATU 291 (see the beginning of this note), although none of them cannot be read KID. The correct reading and meaning of the sign T 34 remains unknown.

2) T 28 ☰ and T 29 ⊕ – representing, in all probability, the excrements of goats and sheep; after the further process of drying and formation, they have been used as a fuel (see FSTW, p. 135). The token type 3:52 ⊕ could be compared with the sign T 29.

Other signs appearing in the archaic registers of garments/cloths i.e. T 10 to T 17, T 35 and T 36 remain not identified.

The results of the analysis of the data inserted into Table II and Table III, can be formulated, as follows: the number of tablets examined in this chapter amounts 112: 35 from Uruk (IV), 46 from Uruk (III), 22 from Jemdet Nasr, 8 – from Uqair, one – of unknown provenience. The statistic data in relation to the archaic times are not completely representative, however the archaic tablets found especially in Uruk, can be accepted in some measure representative to draw some conclusions. Nearly all the archaic tablets come from the Eana district, and were found in the level Uruk IV-III dating to about 3200-3000/2900 B.C. This area was precisely examined, thus we can assume that almost the majority of archaic tablets deriving from this district offer the majority of most characteristic documents concerned with the archaic socio-economic life.[58]

The items: T 27, T 28, T 29, T 37 (fleece), and T 38 (wool) are not included in this analysis (T 37 and T 38 – see Chapter II).

The majority of garments and cloths were designated in archaic documents by single signs.

The furry skirt T 1 (LAL) had been registered in Uruk (IV) 14 times, in Uruk (III) – 17 times, in Jemdet Nasr – 18 times, in Uqair 2 times, all together in 51 entries.

The high frequency is observed also for clothing t u g₂, but in different disposition: in Uruk (IV) t u g₂ appears only 7 times, in

---

[58] From among 35 tablets from Uruk (IV) – 16 were found in the region of the "Limestone Temple", and on the terrain of the so-called "Red Temple", 15 – on the area of the "Great Court" or near by, the remaining 4 tablets – in various sites of the district Eana. From among 46 tablets from Uruk (III) – 20 were found behind the south corner of the "Great Court", 6 – on its terrain, 11 – on the area of the "Stampflehm Building", the remaining 6 tablets – in various sites in the region of the precinct Eana, and 3 – behind it. The plan of the district Eana in archaic Uruk – see ZATU, p. 28 and ATU-3, pp. 13, 14 and 15.

Uruk (III) as many as 21 times, in Jemdet Nasr only 3 times, and in Uqair 4 times, all together in 35 entries. Noteworthy is the fact of nearly equal number of entries including the skirt LAL in (Uruk (IV), Uruk (III) and Jemdet Nasr; on the contrary – the higher notation of the clothing t u g_2 in Uruk (III) than in Uruk (IV) and Jemdet Nasr.

The unidentified artifact T 17 has been often registered, on the whole 24 times, in almost equal numbers in the three cities: Uruk, Jemdet Nasr and Uqair.

The artifacts made of flax g a d a (T 3) have been registered in Uruk (IV) 5 times, in Uruk (III) – 8 times, in Uqair – 5 times, they are absent in Jemdet Nasr.

The sign T 16 (ME) appears almost proportionally in the registers of three cities, on the whole 17 times, among them 7 times in Uruk (IV).

The artifact T 20 appears in Uruk (IV) accounts 6 times, in the Uruk (III) – 4 times, in Uqair – once, but it is absent in Jemdet Nasr.

The artifact T 24 is attested 10 times only in Uruk (III).

In addition I can quote the artifact T 14 registered in Uruk (III) texts 9 times; T 6 and T 7 designating two similar artifacts – only in Uruk (IV) – together 8 times; T 13 is attested 7 times: (in Uruk (IV) – twice, in Uruk (III) – 4 times, in Jemdet Nasr – once).

The remaining garments/cloths appear in the textile registers only occasionally in Uruk (IV) and Uruk (III), once in Jemdet Nasr (these observations concern artifacts: T 5; T 8; T 9; T 10; T 11; T 19; T 22; T 30 – see Table III).

The following garments/cloths have been recorded only in Uruk (IV) texts: T 6; T 7; T 9; T 12; T 23; T 32; T 35 and T 36.

The following garments/cloths have been recorded only in Uruk (III) texts: T 4; T 14; T 15; T 21; T 24 to T 29, T 33 and T 34.

The designation s u m u n "old, used" needs a special interpretation. It appears always directly after the preceding entry which includes the registration of an artifact made of hide or textile. I assume that sumun indicates in that case the old or used hide/textile recorded in the preceding entry, without repeating its name (see n. 30). The designation   s u m u n   follows, first of all, the furry skirt T 1 (LAL): 6 times in the Uruk texts, but as many as 15 times in Jemdet Nasr. Moreover   s u m u n   appears   5   times after the artifact T 6, once after T 9, and once after T 17 (all these artifacts remain unidentified).

The signs which accompany the sings of garments/cloths, cause another problem. I have already interpreted the possible meaning of the additional signs, as: the title e n; BUR_2; signs UD/ b a b b a r, NE, GIG_2, GI/DAR and $DARA_4$ – designating various colours, as well as: T 16 (ME); T 15 (AŠ); NA_2; GAL; SAG; ERIM. But there are signs: BA, ZATU 749 and DUR_2 (see Table III), which also accompany the textile/hide artifacts.

The sign BA read   b a   is of special interest: it designates "allotment" in the system of rationing of various goods to respective persons. The sign BA appears in the archaic economic texts beside the following artifacts: T 18 (t u g_2); T 18 (t u g_2)-BUR_2; T 19; T 20; T 22 (cf. A. Waetzoldt, *Untersuchugen zur Neusumerischen Textilindustrie*, Roma 1972, pp. 84-88 "Stoffrationen", especially p. 87 – allotments of wool and clothing   s i g_2 - b a   and   t u g_2 - b a).[59]

The sign ZATU 749 𝄢 unidentified, appears in the archaic economic texts once beside the clothing t u g_2 on the tablet W 20274,95 from Uruk (III) – see Table II and Table III.

DUR_2 ⊕ latter written $^{g i š}$d u r_2 - r a, indicates a part of loom (see A. Salonen, op.cit., p.162), and appears in Uqair only once, be-

---

[59] Already in the pre-sargonic period definite persons – officials, workers – have received the allotments of wool and cloth. The allotments designated: t u g_2 - b a concerned cloth, not a garment. This interpretation was based on the accounts from the Ur III period, as, for example: 1/2 t u g_2 u š - b a r   t u g_2 b a - PN - a s l a g = "a half of the cloth t u g_2 (for the garment) u š - b a r , the allotment b a (of the cloth) tug_2 for PN – "fuller". The allotment of a half of a garment is impossible. The similar manner of counting appears by allotments of the flax textiles: i g i - 4 - g a l_2 g a d a = "1/4 cloth of flax" (see H. Waetzoldt, op.cit., p. 84 and p. 84 n. 345). Apart of the system of allotments of cloth by pieces, their weight were sometimes quoted in the documents from the Ur III period – to designate the exact dimension of each piece of a cloth (see H. Waetzoldt, op.cit., p. 86 and p. 86, n. 350).

side bag/sack T 31 (BARA$_2$) – see MSVO-4, 26, Pl. 14. This compound is not clear.

The additional three designations mentioned above appear rarely in the Uruk (IV) documents, more often in the Uruk (III) records, in Jemdet Nasr – rarely, in Uqair singly (see Table III).

The more detailed descriptions of the hide/textile artifacts in the Uruk (III) period are not surprising because of the general development of the socio-economic life in this period, followed by rich development of various branches of handicraft. With regard to the textile production it concerned especially the textile/clothing t u g$_2$, which in course of time became more and more differentiated in quality and fashion, but remained the most popular woolen cloth suit various modifications.

Representations of garments revealed by the archaeological monuments are not numerous, but even these from the first half of the third millennium B.C., and also the little later, permit the comparison with clothings described in the archaic documents. First of all, several monuments show the furry skirt LAL (?) worn by various persons/dignitaries (see p. 46, Figs. 9-11).

The sleek skirts with wisps at their lower end are presented by several statuettes or in reliefs, the clothing t u g$_2$ can be also recognized in some of them: (see pp. 47-48, Figs. 12-17).

At the end, I would like to emphasise that garments and cloths used by the ethnically close group of people, preserve generally – for a long time – their traditional shapes.

Examples of textile records   (outline copies)

Uruk IV

W 9578 h, obv.

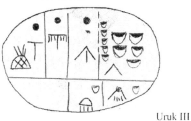

W 9312 n2+r,   obv.

Uruk III

W 20274,30, obv.

W 20274,97, obv.

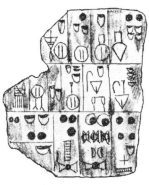

Jemdet Nasr

MSVO-1, 179

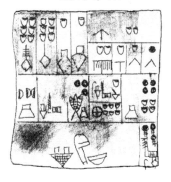

Uqair

MSVO-4, 25

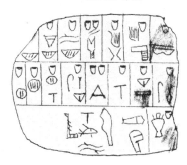

The furry skirts of the pelt $^{k u š}$LAL (?)

Fig. 9
Sumerian priest-adorer

Fig. 10
King from Mari

Fig. 11
Warriors from Lagaš

Skirts of sleek hide or cloth, with wisps at their ends

Fig. 12
Adorer from Tell Asmar (Ešnunna)

Fig. 13
Adorers from Khafadje

Fig. 14. Fragment of the so-called "Standard from Ur"

48

The woolen clothing t u g₂ put on the whole body through the left shoulder

Fig. 15
Couple in courting mien
from Nibru/Nippur,
the woman in the clothing t u g₂

Fig. 17
The king Eanatum from Lagaš
at the head of this troops.
The clothing t u g₂ put on
the furry skin.

Fig. 16
Sumerian Lady from
Tell Asmar (Ešnunna)

TABLE I
Archaic Sumerian signs appearing in records of garments and cloths

Sign T-no.	Pictograph	Token type-no	Sign number in: ATU-1	ZATU	Jemdet Nasr (Pl)
1	2	3	4	5	6
T1		8:1 ?	388	307;534	270
T2		8:11 ?	389	644	271
T3			401/402	186	–
T4			–	186	–
T5			–	187	–
T6	,	10:4 *	409/410; 390	662	–
		8:7 ?			
T7			829/830	663	–
T8		8:8 ?	717	662	–
T9		8:29 ?	(717)	663	–
T10		10:12 *	682	534	158
T11		10:13 *	685	644	–
T12		10:9 *	–	662	–
T13	,		690	418	58/48[?]
T14			222+21+684	37+449+51	–
T15			222	37	1
T16		(10:9)?	487	358	314
T17		10:10 ?	555	753	408
T18		3:28 *	755	555	390_1
T19		3:20 *	758	452-b	–
		3:29			
T20		3:30 *	759/798[?]	452-e;-b	–
		3:21 *			

50

(Table I – p. 2)

T21	⊕	3:32 ⊕ * –		452-e	–
		3:33 ⊕			
T22	⊕	3:22 ⊕ * –		452-b	–
		3:24 ⊕			
T23	⊕	3:24/25 ⊕ * –		453	–
T24	⊕		–	556	–
T25	⊕	3:39 ⊕ ? –		557	–
T26	⊕		–	558	–
T27	⋈		–	184	
T28	+		234+508	516	–
T29	⊕	3:52 ⊕ *	761+508	516	–
T30	⊒⊏		519	759	–
T31	⊠	7:17 ⊠ ?	588	52-a	–
T32	⊞	7:18 ⊞ *	589/590?	764	–
T33	⊞	7:5 ⊡ ?	–	764	–
T34	⊓		–	291-a (U.III)	–
T35	⌂		–	85	251
T36	⌂		–	691	–
T37	⊟⊟ , ⊟⊟	4:21 ⊟⊟ ?	(523)	73-c	385
		4:29 ⊟⊟ ?			
T38	⊕ , ⊕	3:55 ⊕ *	801,757	452-a	385
		3:56 ⊕			

- * – Identification accepted by D. Schmandt-Besserat in: *How Writing Came About*, 1996
- A small circle on the tokens presents their perforation.

(Tabl. 1 – p. 3)

T-no.	Sign number in:		Identification/reading	
	Ur Archaic	Fara LAK	in this article	in ZATU
	7	8	9	10
T1	292?	756	LAL	ŠU$_2$, LA$_2$/LAL
T2	9	17	TIL (s u m u n)	cf. TIL/UŠ$_2$
T3	217	285	g a d a	g a d a
T4	–	–	–	g a d a
T5	–	–	–	GADA $gunû$
T6	–	–	▬	–
T7	–	–	–	662+U
T8	–	–	▬	–
T9	–	–	▬	662+U
T10	–	–	▬	ŠU$_2$
T11	–	–	–	–
T12	–	–	–	–
T13	79?	131?	–	NU $gunû$
T14	–	–	AŠ+SAL+BAR	AŠ+SAL+BAR
T15	1	1	AŠ	AŠ/RUM
T16	289	750	ME/IŠIB	ME/IŠIB
T17	–	–	–	▬
T18	385 a, c	792	t u g$_2$	t u g$_2$
T19	–	–	▬	SIG$_2$
T20	–	–	▬	SIG$_2$
T21	–	–	▬	SIG$_2$
T22	–	–	▬	SIG$_2$
T23	–	–	▬	SIG$_2$+U

(Table 1 – p. 4)

T24	...	...	...	TUG$_2$+BAD+BAD
T25	–	–	...	TUG$_2$. *gunû*
T26	...	–	–	TUG$_2$ *gunû*+BAD+BAD
T27	...	...	GA'AR$^?$	GA'AR
T28	–	794$^?$	MAŠ-ŠE$_3$	ŠE$_3$-MAŠ
T29	–	...	UDU-ŠE$_3$	ŠE$_3$-UDU
T30	...	...	...	...
T31	–	...	BARA$_2$	BARA$_2$
T32	...	...	...	...
T33	266$^?$	...	...	...
T34	...	...	...	KID-a
T35	...	...	...	DU$_8$ (?)
T36	–	...	...	...
T37	...	793	–	(DARA$_4$?)
T38	–	793	s i g$_2$	s i g$_2$

TABLE II

Tablets with records of garments/cloths

Tablet no.	Findspot arch. level, square	Nos of T-signs and their possible reading

A. Tablets from archaic Uruk

Uruk IV

Tablet no.	Findspot	Nos of T-signs and their possible reading
1. W 6611	Pd XVI-3	1 (LAL)
2. W 6738c	"	1 (LAL)
3. W 6820	"	17; 11
4. W 6881ab	"	6; 2 (s u m u n)
5. W 6882a	"	1 (LAL)
6. W 7024	"	1 (LAL); 2 (s u m u n)
7. W 9123p	Qa XVI-2	20
8. W 9312n$_2$+ r	"	6; 2 (s u m u n); 17; 16 (ME); 1 (LAL) / or: 10
9. W 93351	"	[ ]; 2 (s u m u n); 13; 16 (ME)
10. W 9578h	"	1 (LAL); 2 (s u m u n); 17; 16 (ME); 7; 8; 3 (g a d a)
11. W.9579a	"	7
12. W 9579bi	Pd XVI-3	20
13. W 9579cb	Qa XVI-2	31 (BARA$_2$)
14. W 9579dc	"	1 (LAL)
15. W 9579p	"	18 (t u g$_2$)
16. W 9655b	"	6; 2 (s u m u n)
17. W 9761b	Pb XVI 5	20; 18 (t u g$_2$); 1 (LAL)
18. W 10585	"	20; 5
19. W 19408,40	Nb XVI 3	30
20. W 19408,41	"	16 (ME)
21. W 19408,46	"	23; 22; 8; 10; 17; 1 (LAL); (on the edge sub-script: 18 (t u g$_2$) – GA)
22. W 19408,48	"	17; 16 (ME); 1 (LAL); 30; 35
23. W 19408,55	"	31 (BARA$_2$)
24. W 19408,57	"	16 (ME); 17; 3 (g a d a); 1 (LAL); 13; 30
25. W 19408,60	"	20; 18 (t u g$_2$); 19; 10; 6; 2 (s u m u n); 31 (BARA$_2$); 32
26. W 19410,12	"	7; 6$^?$; 2 (s u m u n): 1 (LAL); 9; 2 (s u m u n); 17
27. W19578b	"	19; 18 (t u g$_2$); 17; 17-EN; 16 (ME); 1 (LAL)
28. W 19584dj	Nc XVI-2	18 (t u g$_2$)
29. W 19637	Nb XVI-3	18 (t u g$_2$); 3 (g a d a); 17; 36
30. W 19684a	Nc XVI-2	18 (t u g $_2$); 20

(Table II – p. 2)

31. W 20044,6	Nc XVI-4	1 (LAL); 1 (LAL) – ERIM$^?$; 1 (LAL)-EN$^?$
32. W 20245	Nb XVI-5	3 (g a d a)
33. W 20650	Ob. XVI-2$^?$	22; 23; 12
34. W 20705	Ob. XVI-4	11
35. W 21278	Nc XVI-5	19; 18 (t u g$_2$)-EN; 3 (g a d a); 31 (BARA$_2$)

Uruk III

1. W 10731	Pa XVI-5	3 (g a d a); 13; 1 (LAL); 20-EN; 18 (t u g$_2$)
2. W 10846	wadis	20 – EN; 18 (t u g$_2$) -EN; 20; 18 (t u g$_2$)
3. W 14777a	Oe XVI-3	1 (LAL); 15 (AŠ)
4. W 15777M	Nc/b XVI-4	18 (t u g$_2$); 3 (g a d a)
5. W 19449	Lb XV-5	1 (LAL); 13; 16 (ME); 17
6. W 20246,1	Nc XVI-5	18 (t u g$_2$); 14; 24; 38 (s i g$_2$) ?
7. W 20246,2	"	1 (LAL); 15 (AŠ); 29
8. W 20274,1	Nc XVII-1	37; 18 (t u g$_2$)
9. W 20274,14	"	[ ]; 2 (s u m u n); 14
10. W 20274,17	"	29
11. W 20274,22	"	18 (t u g$_2$) - BUR$_2$; 18 (t u g$_2$); 1 (LAL); 14; 24
12. W 20274,23	"	31 (BARA$_2$); 33
13. W 20274,26	"	31 (BARA$_2$)
14. W 20274,27	"	14; 18 (t u g$_2$) – 15 (AŠ$^?$); 24; 27; 28
15. W 20274,28	"	18 (t u g$_2$) – BUR$_2$;18 (t u g$_2$); 24; 27; 28
16. W 20274,29	"	18 (t u g$_2$) – 15 (AŠ$^?$); 24; 27$^?$; 28
17. W 20274,30	"	1 (LAL); 15 (AŠ); 18 (t u g$_2$); 18 (t u g$_2$) – BUR$_2$; 14; 18 (tug$_2$) – 15 (AŠ); 24; 29; 28; 27; 38 (s i g$_2$)
18. W 20274,45	"	18 (t u g$_2$); 14; 15 (AŠ)-[ ]; 18 (t u g$_2$)-15 (AŠ); 31 (BARA$_2$)-15(AŠ); 38 (s i g$_2$)$^?$
19. W 20274,77	"	33; 34; 31 (BARA$_2$); 30, 1 (LAL)-UD/b a b b a r (subscript without number)
20. W 20274,80	"	20-EN; 18 (t u g$_2$)- EN; 20- BA; 19- BA; 22$^?$ –BA; 18 (tug$_2$) – BA; 25; 20; 21; 22; 26
21. W 20274,95	"	22-EN; 18 (t u g$_2$)- ZATU 749; 22 - BA ; 18 (t u g $_2$)- BA; 18 (t u g$_2$)- BA- BUR$_2$; 18 (t u g$_2$)- BUR$_2$; 18 (t u g$_2$); 24$^?$; 3 (g a d a)
22. W 20274,97	"	18 (t u g$_2$); 18 (t u g$_2$)- BUR$_2$; 14; 18 (t u g$_2$) – 15 (AŠ); 24; 31 (BARA$_2$); 28
23. W 20274,125	"	31 (BARA$_2$) – 15 (AŠ)$^?$; 24
24. W 20327,1	"	18 (t u g$_2$); 20; 25; 30
25. W 20367,2	Nc XVI-5	31 (BARA$_2$)
26. W 20493,1	Nc XVI-1	31 (BARA$_2$); 33 – NA$_2$; 33 – EZINU
27. W 20493,4	"	1 (LAL); 2 (s u m u n); 3 (g a d a); 17

(Table II – p. 3)

28. W 20494,4	Nc XVII-1	33; 38 (s i g_2)
29. W 20511,1	"	18 (t u g_2); 37
30. W 20511,3	"	18 (t u g_2); 18 (t u g_2)- BUR_2; 14; 1 (LAL);
		24; 28; 27
31. W 20739	Nd XVI-4	18 (t u g_2); 3 (g a d a); 1 (LAL); 2 (s u m u n);
		16; 17; 10; 13
32. W 21026	Nc XVI-5	1 (LAL); 5; 4; 10; 19
33. W 21342	Ne XVII-1	5; 1 (LAL); 11; 26
34. W 21671	Ob.XVI-1	1 (LAL); 20; 18 (t u g_2); 3 (g a d a); 31 ($BARA_2$)
		(the first four items are summed up)
35. W 21736	Oc XV-4	8; 10; 1 (LAL); 2 (s u m u n); 19
36. W 21912	Ob XV-4	17; 18 (t u g_2)
37. W 21913	"	22; 17; 3 (g a d a)
38. W 23851	Ob XV-3	[ ]; 2 (s u m u n); 3 (g a d a)
39. W 23951	Ob XV-4	18 (t u g_2); 1 (LAL)
40. W 23969,1	Ob XV-3	29
41. W 23988	"	1 (LAL) or 10; 13; 15 (AŠ)$^?$
42. W 24008,20	Ob/c XV-4	37; 1 (LAL); 2 (s u m u n); 3 (g a d a); 16; 17
43. W 24012,4	Ob XV-3	18 (t u g_2); 3 (g a d a)-GAL; 1 (LAL); 14
44. W 24024,1	"	16 (ME); 1 (LAL); 17; 2 (s u m u n); 30- SAG;
		16 (ME)-17; 3 (g a d a); 18 (t u g_2)
45. W 24046,4	Oc XV-4	24; 31 ($BARA_2$); 18 (t u g_2); 20
46. MSVO-4,68	from Uruk ?	31 ($BARA_2$)

B. Tablets from Jemdet Nasr

MSVO-1, tablet no.:

1. 46 (Pl. 17)	small fragment	[ ]; 2 (s u m u n)
2. 70 (Pl. 25)	" "	18 (t u g_2);
3. 83 (Pl. 30)		1 (LAL); 2 (s u m u n); 16 (ME); 17
4. 93 (Pl. 33)		1 (LAL); 2 (s u m u n); 17
5. 94 (Pl. 34)		1 (LAL); 2 (s u m u n)
6. 95 (Pl. 34)		1 (LAL); 2 (s u m u n)
7. 96 (Pl. 35)		1 (LAL); 2 (s u m u n); 16 ME – 17
8. 97 (Pl. 35)		1 (LAL); 16 (ME)-17; 1 (LAL); 2 (s u m u n)
9. 98 (Pl. 35)		1 (LAL); 2 (s u m u n); [ ]$^?$- 17
10. 103 (Pl. 37)		1 (LAL); 2 (s u m u n); 17
11. 108 (Pl. 38)		1 (LAL); 2 (s u m u n); 16 (ME)
12. 109 (Pl. 40)		1 (LAL); 2 (s u m u n); 16 (ME) – 17
13. 111 (Pl. 42)		1 (LAL); 2 (s u m u n); 17
14. 116 (Pl. 45)		13$^?$ (subscript after col. I)

(Table II – p. 4)

15. 117 (Pl. 45)	1 (LAL)
16. 127 (Pl. 48)	1 (LAL); 2 (s u m u n)
17. 130 (Pl. 49)	30; 1 (LAL); 2 (s u m u n); 17
18. 135 (Pl. 51)	1 (LAL); 17
19. 160 (Pl. 58)	1 (LAL); 2 (s u m u n); 16 (ME)
20. 177 (Pl. 68)	1 (LAL); 2 (s u m u n); 17 –16 (ME)
21. 179 (Pl. 70)	[ ]; 2 (s u m u n); 1 (LAL); [ ]-1 (LAL); 16 (ME); 17
22. 205 (Pl. 77)	18 (t u g$_2$)

C. Tablets from Uqair

MSVO-4, tablet no.:

1. 6 (Pl. 4)	18 (t u g$_2$)
2. 17 (Pl. 8)	3 (g a d a); 18 (t u g$_2$)
3. 18 (Pl. 10)	14$^?$; 17
4. 19 (Pl. 10)	18 (t u g$_2$); 3 (g a d a)
5. 23 (Pl. 11)	16 (ME); 3 (g a d a)
6. 24 (Pl. 12/13)	19; 3 (g a d a); 1 (LAL)
7. 25 (Pl. 12)	16 (ME); 3 (g a d a); 14; 18 (t u g$_2$) – 16 (ME); 20; 18 (t u g$_2$); 19$^?$
8. 26 (Pl. 14)	1 (LAL); 31 (BARA$_2$) – DUR$_2$; 18 (t u g$_2$) –30-SAG

D. Tablet of unknown provenience

MSVO-4, no. 78 (Pl. 40) 1 (LAL)

TABLE III

The frequency of the signs T 1 – T 38
on the archaic Sumerian tablets from
Uruk, Jemdet Nasr and Uqair

T – nos	Uruk IV	Uruk III	Jemdet Nasr	Uqair
1 (LAL)	14 (times)	17	18	2
1 (LAL) EN?	1			
1 (LAL) ERIM?	1			
1 (LAL) UD		1		
2 (s u m u n)	9	7	17	
3 (g a d a)	5	8		5
3 (g a d a) GAL		1		
4		1		
5	1	2		
6	5			
7	3			
8	2	1		
9	1			
10	2	3		
11	2	1		
12	1			
13	2	4	1	
14		9		2?
15 (AŠ)		4		
15 (AŠ) [ ]		1		
16 (ME)	7	4	4	2
16 (ME) 17		1	4	
17	9	7	7	1
17 EN	1			
[ ] 17			1	
18 (t u g $_2$)	7	21	3	4
18 (t u g$_2$) EN	1	2		
„ BUR$_2$		6		
„ 15 (AŠ)		5		
„ BA		2		
„ BA BUR$_2$		1		
„ ZATU 749		1		

(Table III, p. 2)

T – nos	Uruk IV	Uruk III	Jemdet Nasr	Uqair
18 (t u g_2) 16 (ME)				1
" 30 SAG				1
19	3	2		2
19 BA		1		
20	6	4		1
20 EN		2		
20 BA		1		
21		1		
22	2	2		
22 EN		1		
22 BA		1		
23	2			
24		10		
25		2		
26		2		
27		5		
28		5		
29		3		
30	3	2	1	
30 SAG		1		
(cf. t u g_2 30 SAG)				
31 (BARA$_2$)	4	9		
31 (BARA$_2$) 15 (AŠ)		2		
31 (BARA$_2$) DUR$_2$				1
32	1			
33		3		
33 NA$_2$		1		
33 EZINU		1		
34		1		
35	1			
36	1			
37 (fleece ?)		2		
38 (s i g_2)		3		

Table IV

Archaic Sumerian Lexical Lists
concerning garments and cloths

(List "Textilien" – ATU-3, pp. 131-132 included to the list "Vessels"
from item 85 to 116, and single items in some other lists).

List "Vessels":	T-nos.:	Tablets:
85	T 9	W 20266,2; W 20266,33
86	T 9 EN	W 20266: 2; 33; 34
87	T 8	W 20266: 2; 33; 34
88	T 8 EN	W 20266: 2; 33; 143
89	T 20 EN	W 20213,4b; W 24013,14; W 24243,1
90	T 18 (t u g$_2$) EN	W 20213,4b; W 24013,14; W 24243,1
91	T 18 (t u g$_2$) UD	W 20266,2; W 24013,14
92	T 25 (TUG$_2$.gunû) UD	W 20266,2; W 20266,11; W 21158,3
93	T 18 (t u g$_2$) GI$_6$/GIG$_2$	W 20266,2; W 20266,11; W 21158,3
94	T 25 (TUG$_2$.gunû) GI$_6$/GIG$_2$	W 20266,11
95	T 18 (t u g$_2$) GI	W 20266,11
96	T 25 (TUG$_2$.gunû) GI	W 20266,11
97	T 18 (t u g$_2$) NE	W 20266,11
98	T 25 (TUG$_2$.gunû) NE	W 20266,11
99	T 18 (t u g$_2$) NE GAR	W 20266,39
100	T 25 (TUG$_2$.gunû) NE GAR	W 20266,39
101	BUR$_2$ T 18 (t u g$_2$)	W 21735,4
103	TUR-BUR$_2$ T 18 (t u g$_2$)	W 21735,4
104	BUR$_2$ TUR [T 25 (TUG$_2$.gunû)]	W 20266,11
105	DARA$_4$ T 18 (t u g$_2$)	W 21735,4
107	T 15 (AŠ) GIŠ T 18 (t u g$_2$)	W 20266,11; W 21735,4
108	T 15 (AŠ) GIŠ.tenû [ ]	W 20266,11
109	KUŠ T 18 (t u g$_2$)	W 21735,4
111	ŠA$_3$ AB$_2$ [T 18 (t u g$_2$)]	W 20266,33
112	ŠA$_3$ AB$_2$ T 25 (TUG$_2$.gunû)	W 20266,33
113	LUM [A$^?$] T 18 (t u g$_2$)	W 20266,33
114	LUM A T 25 (TUG$_2$.gunû)	W 20266,33
115	3 x T 15 (AŠ) AB$_2$ T 18 (t u g$_2$)	W 20266,33
116	3 x T 15 (AŠ) AB$_2$ [T 25 (TUG$_2$ gunû)]	W 20266,33

List "Vocabulary"-2 – ATU-3, Taf. 80
      T 18 (t u g_2) ?   W 14264

List "Vocabulary"-9 – ATU-3, Taf. 81
      T 1 (LAL); T 15 (AŠ); T 16 (ME); T 13   W 9123 d

List "Vocabulary"-X – ATU-3, Taf. 81
      T 20; T 1 (LAL); T 15 (AŠ); T 3 (g a d a)   W 21002,6

List "Vocabulary"-6, – ATU-3, Taf. 80
      T 20   W 20493,26

List "Metal"-56, – ATU-3, Taf. 73
      T 29 ZATU 777a   W 21208,51

List "Unidentified"-47 – ATU-3, Taf. 93
      T 15 (AŠ);? T 31 (BARA$_2$); T 11; T 1 (LAL)   W 20831,5
              (contd damaged)